The

Looe Island Story

An Illustrated History of St. George's Island

Mike Dunn

ISBN 0 9549137-2-8

Published by
Polperro Heritage Press
Clifton-upon-Teme
Worcestershire WR6 6EN UK
www.polperropress.co.uk

Cover design by Steve Bowgen

Printed by Orphans Press
Leominster HR6 8JT

Foreword

There is something alluring about any island. There is an intriguing privacy, like a glimpse of a courtyard through a street door, or the attractive inscrutability of a lady in a veil. Even on a day trip you are aware of your vulnerability if the weather turns bad or the boatman forgets to collect you. It may feel strange to be dependent on tides to control your coming and going, rather than the clock. This story helps to open the door or lift the veil for anyone wanting to know more about the island to the South West of Looe Harbour entrance.

Mike Dunn struck a rich seam when he started his research into Looe Island and its story. His book, acknowledging the help of the many other contributors, brings together a range of sources from the Charter of 1144 to Babs Atkins' 2004 legacy to the Cornwall Wildlife Trust. He tells stories of smuggling, when tobacco could be sold for more than ten times the cost in Guernsey and the southern shore provided a landing place invisible from the mainland. Little wonder that the 'free traders' took an interest in it. This book is also a practical guide to the island today, including advice against risking Trelawny's island when the gulls are bringing up their chicks.

My family owned the island for nearly 200 years. My own connection dates back to 1944 when it was uninhabited and I landed and made myself ill eating unripe gooseberries. Boys were always hungry in those wartime years. It is about 20 years since I first met the Atkins sisters and was later very touched when they asked me for help to define what sort of successor could meet their aim of 'no development at any price'. The Cornwall Wildlife Trust will keep faith with their legacy.

I am sure others will enjoy reading this book with as much interest as I have.

Sir John Trelawny
March 2005

Acknowledgements

I am indebted to my wife, Jenny, for introducing me to St. George's Island, and the remarkable Atkins sisters. Jenny knew them because the late Evelyn Atkins was a school friend (and later bridesmaid) to her mother 'Tommy' Odd. 'Tommy' met Evelyn in about 1920 when travelling by train to the grammar school they attended in Surrey. They remained lifelong friends and 'Tommy' is mentioned in both Evelyn's books. Both were unusually adventurous for the era and hence the nickname 'Tommy' for a tomboy. As young women they took the then unusual step of embarking on a cruise together on the *S.S. Doric*. 'Tommy' was an instant convert but 'Attie' hated it which is ironic considering that destiny was to inextricably link her life with the sea. It was 'Tommy' who took over Evelyn's job at a coal merchant's office (affectionately known in the family at that time as the 'coal hole') in Epsom when her removal to Cornwall was imminent thus overcoming her desire not to let down the proprietor who had been kind to her.

Without the encouragement and support of 'Babs' Atkins, who kindly loaned some of her papers, including transcriptions of articles relating to Looe from the *Cornish Times* between 1857 and 1905, the project would not have been attempted. I am also grateful for the help provided by the staff of local and national archives.

Of particular value in the early stages was an introduction to local historian Carole Vivian by Ann and Paul Brumpton who run self-catering accommodation in Tremaine, near Pelynt. At short notice, Carole Vivian generously gave of her time and research information thus providing a solid foundation upon which to begin.

More recently Barbara Birchwood-Harper, Curator of the Old Guildhall Museum in Looe and archivist of the Looe Old Cornwall Society has made a very significant contribution. Her diligent research into the confusing history of Looe smuggling in particular, together with her enthusiastic support and wealth of local history knowledge, have been invaluable. Barbara would particularly like to thank Mary Philp, Jennie Widdowson,

Margaret England, Sarah Haworth, Pam Gyles and John Bailey, all descendants of the Hooper family, George Pritchard and her patient, methodical husband, Neil who has been so supportive and enthusiastic during the whole project.

Particularly helpful information has also been provided by the Royal Institution of Cornwall, Malcolm S. Dann (his ancestors engaged in smuggling) and James P. Derriman who has done much research into the history of the Looe area. My mother, Kathleen I. Dunn, has also given generously of her time and advice sifting through archive material. Mention must also be made of Wren Toms who did so much to help the sisters when they moved to the island, Attie's neice Cecily and her husband Doug Penhaligon who also helped the Atkins' sisters in the early days and more recently have supplied me with family information. Also Tony Pengelly who took over from his grandfather Leonard as supply boatman bringing mail and supplies to the island every week, weather permitting, and the Looe lifeboat crew who assisted with the interment ceremony for 'Babs' and joined some 150 friends and relatives at her memorial service at St. Martins Church, Looe in May 2004.

I am especially grateful to Gus and Sheila Ravine without whom 'Babs' Atkins would have been alone and vulnerable on the island following the death of her sister. They have enthusiastically embraced island life since becoming resident in Smuggler's Cottage, maintained the services and added the boon of Internet communication. Without them, completing this work would have been extremely difficult. For the Cornwall Wildlife Trust, Callum Deveney, Reserve Manager has been very supportive and Tony Stebbings delivered a wonderful eulogy at the memorial service for Babs and reassured everyone that the island is in safe hands. Dr Colin Smithers, great nephew to the sisters, has also welcomed this project.

Special thanks are also due to Sir John Trelawny who has always taken a close interest in the island and kindly introduced me to the publisher of this work. He will be maintaining close contact with the Cornwall Wildlife Trust concerning the future of the island. Last, but by no means least, I should like to record my gratitude to Dave Gardner, the recently deceased and greatly missed Looe boatman, for his cheerful willingness to take us to the island whenever conditions permitted.

Mike Dunn
January 2005

Contents

Island House, Volunteer's Hut and Jetty Cottage

Chapter 1

INTRODUCTION

What is it that so fascinates us about islands? If it be romantic stories of smuggling, buried treasure and adventure then St. George's (or Looe Island[1] as it is more commonly known) can boast all three as we shall see. There is also the sense of remoteness and whilst the island is only a short distance off Hannafore Point to the west of Looe it is frequently cut-off, sometimes for long periods, by adverse sea conditions. On more than one occasion Christmas mail and 'good cheer' was delivered by 'Father Christmas' in a helicopter, courtesy of the local media, after a long period of isolation!

Between the mainland and Looe Island there are rocks the highest of which is referred to as Midmain or Magman according to Gilbert's *The Parochial History of Cornwall*, Vol. IV, published in 1838. Traditionally, it is possible to walk to the mainland at Hannafore with dry feet on Good Friday when the sea recedes due to big spring tides but these days it is rarely possible and slippery seaweed makes the trip hazardous.

Most unusually, and perhaps uniquely, the foreshore (area between the mean high and low water marks) is not owned by the Crown and is therefore private property, a fact recorded in the deeds. According to a previous owner of the island this came about in 1873 when the then Prince of Wales (later to become Edward VII) sold the rights to settle a gambling debt!

The magical ambiance that many feel when they step ashore on St. George's helped the musician Andrew Hugill with his compositions and eventually led to him writing *Island Symphony*, copies of which are for sale on CD in Jetty Cottage at the time of writing.

As visitors will quickly discover, it is a stiff climb to the summit of the island but the effort is rewarded by delightful glimpses of the sea, attractive scenery and finally a panoramic view. The seat at the beginning of the climb is an ideal spot for a picnic and looks out over Little Island (now re-named Trelawny's Island) that can be accessed by a small bridge, providing the seagulls are not nesting.

St. George's covers an area of some 22.5 acres, has a circumference of about one mile, and is 150 feet high at the summit. Geologically the rocks in this area are sedimentary i.e. they were laid down in primeval lakes and seas during the Devonian period some 350 million years ago. This pre-dates the Coniferous period that gave rise to today's coal seams in some parts of the country. There is fresh water from a spring below Smuggler's Cottage and after the drought of 1976 it was noted that it took five weeks for the first rains to filter through to it. Because of the maritime climate St. George's rarely experiences frost or snow and, perhaps uniquely amongst English off shore islands, it is now wooded on the lee side resulting in an attractive and varied habitat for wildlife. On a balmy summer day the atmosphere and views as you ascend to the summit have an almost Mediterranean feel. The mild climate is ideal for horticulture and early daffodils were once grown here for the London markets.

In 1964 the island was purchased by the Atkins sisters from Epsom (see chapter 2) in unusual circumstances. As readers of the two books Evelyn Atkins wrote about their experiences will soon discover, island life is not for the faint hearted. During winter gales mountainous seas pound the rocks sending spray and foam right over Island House. In 1974 a storm coincided with the highest tides for 300 years (caused by the conjunction of the planets). On the morning of the high tide, huge seas crashed down on top of the cliffs near Island House but without significant damage. By the following morning, however, the storm had become even more violent and overnight had washed away a large Victorian boathouse behind the beach plus adjacent boats secured to the trees and a barge measuring 25ft by 12ft used for transporting heavy goods. Then the Great Storm of 1987 caused a cliff fall that wrecked the freshwater pumping system and another violent storm in 1989 washed away much of the track up from the beach (now replaced by a concrete ramp). The great storm of October 1987 was by no means the worst to hit the south. In November 1703 winds, in what has become known as the 'Great British Storm', are estimated to have reached 120mph. The newly constructed Eddystone light was destroyed, over 1000 Royal Navy seamen were killed in the Channel and the total loss of life has been estimated at 8000. For anyone on the island at the time it must have been awe-inspiring.

On a small island storms are dramatic, but potentially much more dangerous is fire and visitors are urged to exercise extreme caution. On the one occasion that a clearance bonfire got out of control, Looe firemen came to the rescue by boat. Had sea conditions prevented a landing however, the situation could have become serious.

To assist with the upkeep of the island the Atkins sisters were always dependent upon volunteers and also introduced working holidays for young people, sometimes in pursuit of a Duke of Edinburgh award.

[1] Looe derives from the Cornish 'Logh' meaning sea-lake or estuary. The boating pool in Looe once powered a tide mill

Looe Island in 1890 (above) and (below) today

Chapter 2

THE ATKINS SISTERS

Any introduction to the island would be incomplete without a reference to the remarkable Atkins sisters, Evelyn and Roselyn Alice, better known as 'Attie' and 'Babs', who became the owners in rather unusual circumstances in 1964 after moving to Nos. 1 and 2 Bassett Court, West Looe. The then owner, who was forced to leave through ill health, was so keen to avoid the island being developed as a holiday camp or similar that he granted the sisters a private mortgage, knowing it would be safe in their hands. The asking price, incidentally, was £22,000!

Both were remarkable ladies from Epsom in Surrey. From an early age 'Attie' had an ambition to be an author and was widely read. Prophetically, she also had an ambition from an early age to own an island! As a young woman her interests included the piano, mountaineering, cricket, cycling, hockey, tennis, photography, amateur dramatics and reading. She was a 'Master shot' with a rifle and represented Surrey at the famous Bisley range. Her photographs were used on the covers of a number of magazines and for postcards of Looe.

During WWII 'Attie' became a part time land girl and then joined the Women's Royal Naval Service (WRNS) where, as an officer, she was in charge of between 50 and 100 Wrens at different times. During this period 'Attie' visited the highly secret tunnels under Dover Castle (now open to the public) and even persuaded the crew of a Motor Torpedo Boat (MTB) to let her drive it round Dover Harbour! Her working life was mostly spent with ICI.

Evelyn 'Attie' Atkins

Even those who knew 'Attie' really well may be surprised that to her school friends she was known as 'Pins'. The author's mother-in-law Honora Odd was 'Attie's' lifelong friend. They met age eleven on their first day at grammar school in Wallington, Surrey. The girls were soon using nicknames and Honora, being a tomboy, became 'Tommy' and 'Evelyn became 'Pins', a tease on Atkins to Hat-pins becoming 'Pins'.

In their early twenties these adventurous young women went on a cruise on the *S.S. Doric*. 'Tommy' loved the experience but 'Attie' quickly realised that she disliked cruising which is ironic considering that thirty years later destiny was to inextricably link her life with the sea. When 'Tommy' married in 1937 'Attie' was her bridesmaid and years later it was 'Tommy' who took over 'Attie's' clerical job in a coal merchant's office in Epsom. Thus 'Attie' knew the job was in good hands and she could leave Epsom and move to her dream island with a clear conscience, a degree of loyalty to her employer that might surprise people today.

'Babs' Atkins

'Babs', the younger sister, was the quieter of the two but equally determined and included in her leisure interests wood carving, gardening, bee keeping, stone polishing, crafts, cooking and wine making. Amongst the possessions taken to the island by small boat when they moved there were 40 gallons of home made wine! Friends and family visiting the sisters became familiar with their homemade elderflower 'champagne' which was produced with much ceremony to celebrate their arrival on the island. A recipe for this refreshing drink appears in Appendix 4. Her career was in teaching and she became a deputy head of a large school in Surrey before moving to Cornwall where she was Senior Mistress at Looe Secondary School until she retired.

The sisters had two elder brothers, William Charles Ralph Atkins and Trevor Cooper Atkins who sadly died within a few months of each other in 1937/38.

'Attie' died in 1997 and is buried in the cemetery at West Looe although it is hoped that she may one day be transferred to her beloved island. 'Babs' died in 2004 (she is buried on the island) but the story of these two remarkable sisters buying the island lives on in 'Attie's' book *We Bought An Island* which provides a highly entertaining account of them fulfilling a dream against all the odds. It won them friends all over the World and a large postbag to be answered, especially after a period of enforced isolation. Who else sends letters in envelopes stamped 'Delayed by Gales'?!

With hectic lifestyles as a result of wide ranging interests and the intervention of WWII the sisters never found time for marriage although as young women they enjoyed dances and parties. Amongst 'Attie's ' papers a light hearted hand written agreement with a friend makes it clear that marriage was not a high priority:-

> "We, the undersigned, hereby declare that should Evelyn Atkins be so unwise as to marry she shall dispatch a German Sausage on her wedding day to Ethel Hook, should she be living at that time. If on the other hand Evelyn Atkins does not marry (the age limit being 35 yrs of age) Ethel Hook (subject to her being alive) shall give Evelyn Atkins a bag of doughnuts on her 35th birthday"

History does not record if the doughnuts were ever delivered!!

Evelyn's second book, *Tales From Our Cornish Island* is an entertaining account of the many adventures and problems the sisters faced once established as residents. Both books are available in an omnibus edition that, at the time of writing, can be purchased in Jetty Cottage.

The sisters were also remarkable for their love affair with gadgets, mostly acquired by mail-order. Unfortunately, the salt laden atmosphere did not always treat these kindly and many had a short life before being consigned to the attic, disposal being too difficult on an island. When the electricity supply fails (the island has no mains supply) there is no option but to go down the track to the generator shed, regardless of the weather, and the sisters became adept at revitalising this fickle machine, sometimes with a few well-aimed blows with a wrench!

All supplies, of course (including oil for the generator), have to be manhandled from the delivery boat. The problems do not always end there. A ton of coal, unloaded on to the jetty in half hundred-weight sacks, was swept away overnight by a south easterly gale and beach combing became a regular occupation for sometime afterwards to retrieve as much of the precious fuel as possible! On another occasion, when 'Attie' was living alone on the island whilst 'Babs' continued her teaching career, she had to drag 21 one hundredweight sacks of coal from the beach to Island House, before they were threatened by the next high tide.

It was whilst Babs was still working as a teacher on the mainland that sea conditions prevented her visiting her sister on the island from Christmas to Easter!

To better understand the challenge the sisters faced in those early days it is interesting to note that they had no telephone or radio phone for communication with the mainland. During school term time 'Babs' lived in Bassett Court, West Looe all week and could only communicate with 'Attie' by waving or, in the winter, flashing a light from Hannafore Point. In an emergency passing fishing boats could be hailed with a venerable whale hide megaphone but it was many years before they obtained a radio-telephone. Now, with the advent of mobile telephones, the island even has the luxury of Internet communication.

A boatman has a contract to deliver mail when conditions permit and will throw it ashore if the sea is too rough to permit a landing.

Island House

That the Atkins sisters were very special and self-sufficient is evident which is perhaps not surprising when one considers their father, William John Edwin Atkins. When only 13, he ran away to sea in the age of sail and rounded Cape Horn, enduring the hazards of manning the yardarms in mountainous seas. After formal training as a seaman his taste for adventure took him to America where he hoboed across the continent, clinging to trains, and even took a job as a cowboy; it seems that adventure was in the Atkins genes!

In 2000, despite very substantial cash offers, 'Babs' ensured the continued conservation of the island by bequeathing it to the Cornwall Wildlife Trust, a selfless act that her sister 'Attie' would have applauded.

The Trust began to take control in 2004, following the death of 'Babs', and quickly began opening new paths and restoring some of the buildings. When funds allow they hope to turn the main building, Island House, into a wildlife centre to be called the Atkins Observatory. Amongst the possessions the Atkins sisters left in the house was a 19th century American-made organ they purchased many years ago from an antique dealer in Looe. It was originally used in Talland church but became redundant when an electrically driven instrument was installed. As Talland church shares with the island links with smuggling and Glastonbury it seems fitting that it came here.

Tommy Odd (left) with 'Attie' (centre) and 'Babs'.

Tommy Odd and 'Attie' with the author (right).

Chapter 3

VISITOR TOUR

The island is usually opened to visitors at Easter subject, of course, to weather and tide conditions. Trips depart from the East Looe Quay at a point by the Fish Market ferry steps where an advertising board will be found advising departure times and a note book for making an advance reservation. The licensed boatman (Tim Corkhill at the time of writing, who is also the Town Crier for Looe) will advise you if tide conditions necessitate using a different departure point.

Until the redoubtable Atkins sisters purchased the island it was not open to visitors and it could well have remained that way. However, in an effort to deter trespassers, whom they did not wish to offend if they were local, the sisters hit upon the idea of a landing fee of 2/6d to discourage them. Far from being discouraging this opportunity to see the island legitimately was welcomed by locals and visitors alike to the point where numbers had to be controlled by licensing just one boatman for the trip. It also led to the introduction of working holidays for volunteers during the summer holidays so that the sisters could devote more time to entertaining visitors. When ex D-Day commander, Major General Rawlins owned the island he discouraged 'visitors' by discharging a shotgun over their heads!

Approaching the jetty

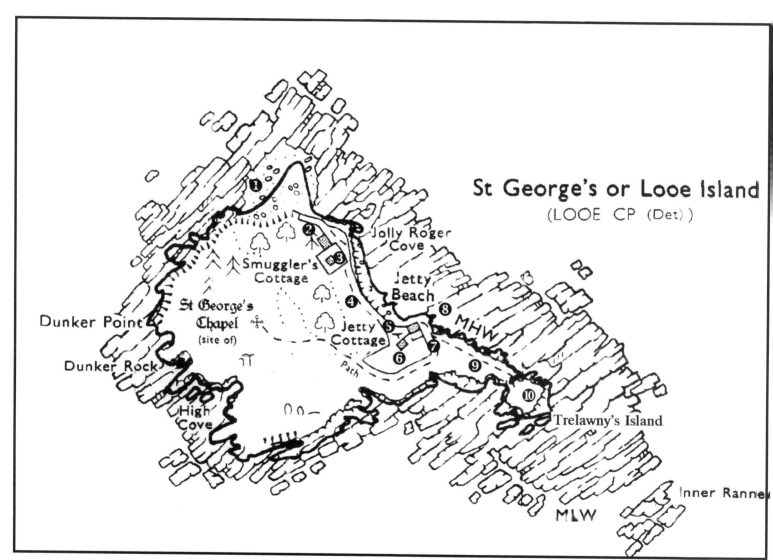

St George's or Looe Island

(LOOE CP (Det))

Jolly Roger Cove

Jetty Beach

Smuggler's Cottage

Dunker Point

St George's Chapel (site of)

Jetty Cottage

Dunker Rock

MHW

High Cove

Path

Trelawny's Island

Inner Ranne

MLW

MHW = Mean High Water
MLW = Mean Low Water

20

Visitors will normally be landed on the main beach (**Point 1** on map) by the boatman, disembarking onto a small landing plank wheeled into positioned by one of the helpers resident on the island. There is also a jetty (**Point 8**). Although the channel to the jetty was deepened by chipping away the rock with pick axes when the Atkins sisters first moved to the island it is only accessible around high tide and is usually used when seas running from a westerly direction make a beach landing hazardous. When the Atkins sisters first came to the island the boat that transported their possessions was too big to land safely in most conditions and it was therefore necessary to transfer to a dingy and row ashore. This could be a hazardous business and on an early visit a sudden lurch as the dingy was pulled ashore sent 'Babs' head over heels over the stern into a winter sea whilst clutching her sister's new Pentax camera!

From the beach, visitors walk up a fairly steep track, the bottom portion of which has twice been washed away by storms. Until 1974 a Victorian Boathouse measuring some 30ft by 12ft stood under the cliffs behind the beach together with a substantial barge that had been used for ferrying machinery and furniture to the island. Then the highest tide for some 300 years coincided with a storm that washed both away together with a section of the cliff beneath Smuggler's Cottage leaving a steep drop to the beach! Even boats secured to the trees disappeared leaving frayed pieces of rope as the only evidence that they had once been there.

Most of the supplies, including drums of diesel oil for the generator, are landed on the beach and, until the recent acquisition of a Quad-Bike, they had to be manhandled up the track. Island life is hard work!

The shed on the right as you walk up the track (**Point 2**), was once used by 'Attie' as a pottery and the next building, clearly identified by the rhythmic beat of a diesel engine, houses the temperamental generator. When functioning correctly it starts automatically whenever a light switch or appliance is switched on in one of the houses.

The track then passes Smuggler's Cottage (**Point 3**). Although today it nestles in the woods, drawings and contemporary accounts reveal a more open aspect during the first quarter of the 19th Century. Indeed the local historian Thomas Bond speculated about the best way to get trees to grow on the island in his 1823 book on the history of Looe. When storms caused a major cliff fall at this point the track to the beach became unsafe and the only supply of fresh water became inaccessible. Technically this was an 'Act of God' and therefore not covered by insurance but as Attie related, a tree trunk fell into the well for which God was not held responsible. The insurance assessor therefore allowed 25% of the cost of moving the fall and re-stabilising the cliff.

Continuing beyond Smuggler's Cottage, with glimpses of Looe Bay, Whitsand Bay and the mainland through the trees to the left, the path passes an area on the right where early daffodils were grown (**Point 4**) and harvested for the London markets when the Atkins sisters first moved to St. George's. 'Babs' is now buried in these fields. In the 19th century the island was quite extensively farmed and the subsequent introduction of some 15 varieties of daffodil, covering an area of about five acres, took advantage of the virtual absence of frost here. It is even said locally that the island is warmer than the nearby mainland and daffodils usually begin blooming in January. A rich winter harvest of seaweed washed up by storms was used to improve the soil each year and suppress weeds.

Smuggler's Cottage

The track finally emerges into an open area with a small market garden on the right (**Point 5**) for fresh provisions in season. Island House (**Point 6**), the main dwelling on the island is ahead and Jetty Cottage to the left. Depending upon the weather visitors are currently met here for an introductory talk or taken directly to Jetty Cottage (**Point 7**) where postcards and books can be purchased to help bolster the island maintenance fund. It is perhaps worth mentioning at this juncture that the island is subject to the highest band Council Tax but receives no services apart from a supply of bin bags that are not collected when full! If you just consider for one moment how much refuse your home produces each week you will realise that one of the biggest problems of island life is disposal of household waste and worn equipment.

Jetty Cottage was originally an old barn and concealed one of the hiding places used by smugglers. When the Atkins sisters first moved to St. George's it became a clearing-house for their possessions, many of which proved unsuitable for island life and found their way into the loft where they remained for over 30 years. The huge bookcase, which at the time of writing is still in Jetty cottage, belonged to the Atkins sisters and getting it here strapped to the top of a small boat when they took up residence early in 1965 was the talk of Looe for a long time.

The Atkins sisters practised many crafts and hobbies here in earlier years, including cutting and polishing the many beautiful stones to be found on the beaches, and established a craft shop in Jetty Cottage. 'Attie' became a keen photographer and many of her pictures were used by magazine publishers and postcard producers. Outside Jetty Cottage there is a seat in a small sun-trap where date palms grow but the more energetic visitors are encouraged to explore the island.

Recently a stock fence has been erected right across the island and a small flock of Hebridean sheep introduced (despite their horns they are harmless!). This does not, however, prevent access to any of the footpaths signposted from Jetty Cottage (**for your safety please keep to marked paths**). Many visitors first walk out beyond the flagpole (**Point 9**) where the Atkins sisters raised the flag of St. George every 23rd April (St. George's Day), and across a small bridge to Little Island, now re-named Trelawny's Island (**Point 10**) by 'Babs' in honour of the famous Cornish family that once owned St. George's and lived at Trelawne Manor, Pelynt, near Looe. Be careful to avoid the blow-hole caused by erosion on your right just before the bridge and note that Trelawny's Island is not accessible when the seagulls are breeding (for their protection and yours!). The rocks that stretch into the sea from Trelawny's Island are the Inner and Outer Ranneys and at low tide there is a natural swimming pool here. In September 2003, Trinity House placed a buoy in the sea off the Ranneys to warn shipping of these hazardous rocks.

From here retrace your steps across the bridge and walk towards the main house (Island House, thought to have been built c1876), keeping the sea to your left and join a path that goes uphill to the left of the house. In a short distance there is a seat on the left with lovely sea views that makes an ideal spot for a picnic before continuing steeply uphill towards the summit of the island that is some 150ft above sea level. The two carved

Chapel site near summit.

stones that are the only visible remains of the Benedictine chapel (**Point 11**) that once stood here are in a small hollow near the summit (**Point 12**) and there are extensive views of the mainland to the north and west. It is said that the bones of a tall man were found here c1783. On a really clear day it is possible to see the Lizard peninsula to the west. To the seaward, some 12.5 miles distant, is the Eddystone Rock on which a lighthouse has existed since 1698. The original, which housed a candelabra burning sixty candles, was swept away in a storm in November 1703 with the inventor inside. The current light, opened in 1882, is visible on clear days.

Places on the summit of the island were, inevitably, in great demand for the historic total solar eclipse at 11am on 11th August 1999. Regrettably, the fickle British climate intervened and cloud cover all but obscured the event in Cornwall.

From the summit there is a choice of paths back to Jetty Cottage, either through the woods or steeply downhill towards Dunker Point and the mainland side of the island but be warned that the latter is steep and slippery in places. Both of these paths emerge on the track to the landing beach close to the generator building. The path by which you ascended is safer and easier. If you choose to retrace your steps, follow the path to the bottom of the hill where it skirts the garden of Island House. The lawn here is man-made and the only level area on the island having been prepared for croquet. During winter storms it can be covered in foam from the raging seas that pound the nearby rocks. In an emergency it is invaluable as a helicopter landing pad. Continuing round the perimeter of the garden, the path returns you to Jetty Cottage.

NB. The paths are subject to change or closure. Please follow any directions given locally and, **for your own safety**, always keep to the paths.

Chapter 4

THE NAME

The earliest recorded name is 'Lamene', which is mentioned in a document from Pope Lucius II in 1144 and the origins of this are discussed in Chapter 6. Over time there have been many variations in the spelling but 'Lammana', which appeared as early as about 1200, is the most common. As recently as 1839 a tithe award on the mainland mentions a hamlet called Lemain and a field called Lemain Park.

By the mid to late 13th century references appear to the island as 'St. Michael of Lammana' and in 1490 a document includes Looe in the name 'Insula Sanctis Micharlis de Loo.' There were, however, inconsistencies:

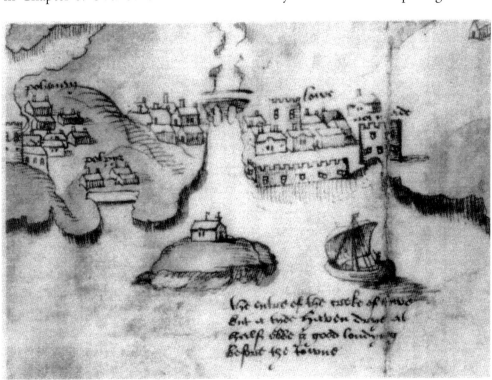

Tudor map of Looe showing chapel on island.

NAME	SOURCE	PERIOD
St. Michael of Lammana	Charter	c1200
Lammana	Court case	1290
St. Nicholas Isle	John Leland	1534 – 1543
The Isle of Lemayne		c1547
Island of St. Michaels		1576
St. Michaels Insul	Christopher Saxton's map	1579
St. Georges Island	Norden	1584
St. Georges	Carew	1602
St. Michaels Island	William Kip's map	1607
St. Michaell's Isle	John Speed's map	1611
St. Michaels Insul	Web's amendment of Saxton's map	1645
St. Michaells Isle	Jan Blaeu's map	1645
St. Michaells Isle	Jan Jansson's map	1646
St Michaels Island	John Adam's Map	c1695[1]
Loos Island		1699
St. Michaels Insul	Richard Blome's map	1715
St. Michael	Herman Moll's map	1724
Island of St. Michael of Lammana		1727
Looe Island	Thos Martyn	1748[2]
Looe Island	Thomas Kitchen's map	1755
Loo Island	Rev Stebbing Shaw	1788
Love [sic]Island	J. Wilke's map	1810
Looe Island	J.C & M Harding	1813
Looe Island	Bond	1823
St. George's or Looe I.	James Pigot & Co's map	1831
Looe Island	Wilkie Collins	1851

There is much speculation as to why the island came to be called St. George's but a reference to a St. George's Feast at Looe in the book *Tudor Cornwall* by the historian A.L. Rowse may be significant:-

"Wherever Kendall[3] was there was trouble. On one St. George's Feast at Looe he came to blows with John Amadas who was there as Commissioner to inquire into a robbery at sea committed by some of the inhabitants upon a Breton boat. Amadas accused him of breaking the peace, accompanied by a crowd of riotous persons. Kendall explained that there was "great resort of all the country thereabouts for their pilgrimage to an image of St. George and that he himself had come there to hear mass with his wife, attended only by a serving lad, not knowing that the Commissioners were meeting there. At their encounter high words passed between him and Amadas, and the latter laid it against Kendall that he had assembled the people."

Where was this 'image of St. George'?! Contemporary documents in the National Archives, Kew, relating to the colleges and chantries state:-

"Tallane. The chainntre called Lamane in ye Isle of Laman. Founded by the Earl of Exeter to fynd a priest to celebrate in a chappel in a little ilande and distante from the paroche church of Talland half a myle."

NB. A parcel of land was sometimes described as 'island' so the use of the term 'isle' above does not necessarily equate with today's understanding of the word.

One might infer from the name St. George's Island that this is where the image was kept but against this the chapel on the mainland was far more convenient especially if large numbers of people were to make a pilgrimage there.

[1] This map can be seen in a National Trust property called 'The Vyne' near Basingstoke, Hants. St. Michael the Archangel is traditionally regarded as the patron saint of many high places such as St. Michael's Mount and the chapel on Rame Head.

[2] The map is in Lanhydrock House Cornwall [National Trust]

[3] William Kendall has been described as a 'restless, scheming man'. Emissaries of the court committed him to the Tower of London in 1531 for causing unrest in Cornwall but he was later released. John Amadas was the King's Serjeant and servant of Cromwell.

Chapter 5

OWNERS & TRAVELLERS' DIARIES

Tracing the secular history of the island is not easy. There is no reference to it in Domesday and, being ex parochial, a normally fruitful source of historical information is not available to us. The diaries of various travellers who passed through Looe and noted the island have however survived and provide some insight into past ownership and residents.

16th to 18th century:
One of the earliest of these comes from rough notes of two or more tours of Cornwall made by John Leland the antiquary between 1534 and 1543. These were edited and combined to form a single account by Alan Gibson for the 1967 reprint of a book 'Early Tours in Devon and Cornwall' by R. Pearse Chope (originally published in 1918). John Leland's Notes on Looe and St. Nicholas Isle (St. George's) merit reproduction in full in the language and variable spelling of the period. The entry for Looe commences with his departure from Polperro (which he calls Poul Pyrre):

> "In the Est Syde also of this Poul Pyrre, ii. Myles of, is another Creeke cawled Loow [sic], being but a Tyde Creke. For at Low water benethe the Bridge a Man may both wade and ryde over yn the Somer. Ther is on eyther Side of this smawl Creke a smaule Fissher Villag, hard on the Se Shore, the one cawlled Est and the other West Loowe, East Loowe being a praty Market Towne and yn eyther of them a Chapel. Also yn the sayde Creekes Mouth neere sumwhat to the Sowthe West is a low Isle cauled S. Nicholas Isle, not a

Quarter of a Myle fro the mayne Shore, and [it] conteyneth a vj. or viij. Acres yn Cumpace, and fedeth Shepe and Cones [rabbits], nurishing also Broode of Se Byrdes."

Leland then continues by refering to the towns of Looe:

"Ther is a great Bridg sumwhat above these ii. Vyllages of x. or xij. Stones Arches, over which the Men passe when the Se ys yn."

It is assumed that the island passed to the crown in 1538 following the dissolution of the monasteries but it is not clear when it passed to Mayow of Bray. We do know that by 1600 Elizabeth I needed to raise money and sold land (Trelawne estate) to Sir John Trelawny.

Another 16th century traveller, Richard Carew of Antony [near Torpoint], referring to St. George's Island, as he called it, observed:

"plentifully stocked with conies [rabbits], in season many seabirds nest here, at which time repairing thither you see your head with a cloud of old ones through their diversified cries witnessing their great dislike of your disturbance and your feet pestered with a large number of young ones formerly, some newly and some not yet disclosed at which time (through the leave and kindness of Master May the owner) you make and take your choice".

Anyone who has disturbed the seagulls during the nesting season will be familiar with their "dislike of your disturbance" but from a historical perspective it is the reference to the owner that is of interest. 'Master May' was almost certainly Philip Mayow (who also owned property at Polruan and held shares in vessels trading to France and Spain) and the island was still in the hands of this family in 1729 (as a 1743 copy of a 1729 indenture preserved in the Cornwall Record Office reveals). In this Philip Mayow of Bray transfers his properties ('Messuages, Island, Lands, Tenements') to his only son and heir, Burthogge Mayow, "in consideration of the sum of £500 of lawful money of Great Britain". The indenture goes on to identify the properties in greater detail including "that Capital Messuage Farm and demesne of lands of or called Bray" and "for all that Island called Looe Island situate, lying and being near the Burrough [sic] of East Looe".

In a second indenture [also in the Cornwall Record Office, Truro] dated 2nd June 1730 Burthogg Mayow of Bray in the County of Cornwall sold to Benjamin Salmon for £400:

"all that island commonly called or known by the name of Looe Island lying near and unto the Borough of East and West Looe (being in his actual possession now) by virtue of a bargain and sale to him thereof made…."

It goes on to describe the property as:

"All houses, buildings, edifices, lands (containing by estimation 20 acres of land), ways, waters, watering place, immoluments [sic], profits, commodities, privileges and appurtenances whatsoever to the said Island appertaining."

The island was purchased in 1743 by Edward Trelawny, Governor of Jamaica, on behalf of the Trelawny estate.

In his 1788 account of *A Tour to the West of England* the Rev. Stebbing Shaw, who later became rector of Hartshorn, sheds light on the occupation of the island during the third quarter of the 18th century. He makes reference to a man who had been transported to the Mewstone, a tiny island south east of Plymouth Sound, about 14 years earlier and served his sentence of seven years there "without setting foot on other land". Evidently this gave the man a taste for island life because Rev. Shaw continues; "Leaving this habitation to his daughter he went to Loo [sic] Island, about thirty miles further in Cornwall". He adds that the daughter remained at Mewstone "a widow with three children, her husband being lately drowned."

Continuing the narrative of his journey the Rev. Shaw describes East Looe as:

"a small ill-built town on the river Loo, separated only by this water from another still smaller, called after the same manner, West Loo. They are both corporate boroughs, sending two members to parliament."

He describes the scenery as :

"truly picturesque, the river winding between two immense hills, not unlike some parts of the Wye. Opposite the mouth of this river stands the small island of the same name, belonging to Sir Henry Trelawney, whose seat is not far from hence; this at a trifling acknowledgement is inhabited by an old man, mentioned at Mews-Rock, Plymouth, whose name is Finn, and by his own industrious cultivation of wheat and other grain, he reaps a comfortable subsistence. At the proper season of the year, various sea-fowl resort to these rocks for the purpose of incubation".

Looe (1839 engraving)

The entry for this part of the reverend gentleman's journey concludes with him crossing "the bridge of thirteen arches; and passed through West Loo in our way to Lostwithiel."

Ownership of the island transferred from Edward Trelawny to Sir Harry Trelawny in 1756. The Trelawnys [the spelling has changed over the years] are a famous Cornish family who lived at Trelawne Manor near Pelynt from about 1600 until the estate was broken up in the 1920's [it is now a holiday caravan park]. They had access to the sea from their estate down the West Looe river. Memorials to the family can be seen in Pelynt church.

Another reference to the cultivation of the island at this time appears in the account of a voyage in a schooner from Hamble in 1793 by a Hampshire gentleman:

"Opposite the town of Looe is Looe Island, where we called again for lobsters. I had the curiosity to go ashore and look at it. There is only one house on the island, which is inhabited by an old man and his family, consisting of 8 including some grand children, it is about a mile round and is cultivated by the old man who rents it. We came in the midst of harvest and saw them taking in their corn. I called at the house and the old lady regaled me with some barley cakes and some cyder. I was welcome she said to the best her house would afford, the old man said he kept a horse and two cows and told me he thought there were about 22 acres of culpable land in the island... After leaving this island it was soon dark and the weather began to look very thick and unfavourable. We could discern the light from the Eddystone lighthouse, the appearance of the sea was very beautiful as it sparkled like so many diamonds round our vessel. I know not if the sailors look upon this as a presage of bad weather, but it was not long before it blew such a gale and rain so violently that we were obliged to lay to and reef our sails. I looked out of my cabin about 2 o'clock in the morning, for so great was the motion of the vessel that it was impossible to sleep. And the sea ran very high indeed. How thankful was I at this moment that those whom I wished for at other times were not with us."

Ward, Lock & Co's *Guide to Looe, Polperro, Fowey, Falmouth and South Cornwall* published c1948 expands on this a little by adding "A family named Finn lived here for nearly forty years, and are credited with having exterminated its swarms of rabbits and rats by eating them indiscriminately"! It also claims that "a chapel (variously said to be dedicated to St. Michael, St. Nicholas and St. George), and a three-gun battery formerly stood upon the hill, but both have disappeared".

19th Century:

Thomas Bond (1765 – 1837) was the historian of Looe and, for nearly 40 years, Town Clerk of East and West Looe. In his book, *Topographical and Historical Sketches of East and West Looe* published in 1823 he too makes reference to the Finn family saying of Looe Island that it "has been inhabited by one family of the name Finn (who before resided on the Mewstone, Plymouth) for about forty years past". Thus he dates their arrival on the island at c1783. His account also tells us something of the appearance of the island in 1823 and in particular "There is no tree on the island: Sir Harry Trelawny, the owner, sometime since had some firs planted there but they did not grow. Bond then opines prophetically that "Tufts of trees on this Island would have a beautiful effect" and goes on to say "I am told the most likely mode of procuring them would be by raising them from seed on the spot, not by planting trees produced in another soil".

Bond provides more detail about the island in his book including confirmation that it was the Finns' who eat the rabbits and rats commenting that "A rat smothered with onions must no doubt be a delicate dish" and the postscript by way of justifying this experiment "He was a bold man indeed who first ate a raw oyster"! Since he was the Town Clerk in Looe for so many years his account surely carries more weight than most and it is therefore worth quoting more of the text:

"This Island is the largest on the cost [sic] of Cornwall, except some of the Scilly Islands. On the top of it are the remains of some building, which goes by the name of the Chapel. Some years since a remarkably large human skeleton was found in it. This Island is hardly half a mile from the nearest land, upon the ebbs of the equinoctial tides may be termed a peninsula, as at those times people frequently walk over it dry shod [never possible today]. There is a dangerous range of rocks called the Ranny, which runs out into the Sea from the Eastern part of this Island. Before the present inhabitants took possession of this domain, it abounded with rabbits and rats. As to the rats they came from a ship, that many years since ran foul of and was wrecked on the Ranny; before which time, tradition says, there were no rats on this place. The rabbits and rats are now much decreased by the inhabitants of the island catching and eating them... These are the only wild quadrupeds, and there are no reptiles."

Bond then relates Richard Carew's report and confirms that in mentioning 'Master May' he was referring to the then owner, 'Mayow'. Interestingly Bond goes on to say that "at the present time few if any birds frequent the island" and one wonders why this would have been? He concludes by adding that "The only houses on the Island are a small dwelling-house and an out-house, which are situated in the lowest part of the island, and appear antient [sic] buildings. Just below the houses is a spring of fresh water." This latter point establishes that the house to which he refers is Smuggler's Cottage since to this day the island's water source is a spring in a cave below the property. It also suggests that the main house was built after 1823 when Bond's book was published. The Atkins sisters had a faded photograph of the house said to have been taken in 1854 but entries in Harriet Trelawny's diary suggest it is more likely that Island House was built about 1876. By then the island was wooded but the trees were all above a line running along the back wall of Smuggler's Cottage.

Looe Island by moonlight, 1890

Wilkie Collins, the famous Victorian author perhaps best known for his book *The Moonstone*, clearly found the eating of the rats an irresistible tale and recounts what he claims to be 'the true story' of their arrival and demise in his 1851 book *Rambles Beyond the Railway*. The mere thought of eating rats is so repugnant that it is worth quoting this passage from his book in full:

"About a mile out at sea, to the southward of the town [Looe], rises a triangular eminence, called Looe Island. Here, many years ago, a ship was wrecked. Not only were the sailors saved, but several free passengers of the rat species, who got on board, nobody knew how, where or when, were also preserved by their own strenuous exertions, and wisely took up permanent quarters for the future on the terra firma of Looe Island. In process of time, and in obedience to the laws of nature, these rats increased and multiplied exceedingly; and, being confined all round within certain limits by the sea, soon became a palpable nuisance. Destruction was threatened to the agricultural produce of all the small patches of cultivated land on the island – it seemed doubtful whether any man who ventured there by himself, might not share the fate of Bishop Hatto, and be devoured by rats. Under these pressing circumstances, the people of Looe determined to make one united and vehement effort to extirpate the whole colony of invaders. Ordinary means of destruction had been tried already, and without effect. It was said that rats left for dead on the ground had mysteriously revived quicker than they could be picked up and skinned, or flung into the sea. Rats desperately wounded had got away into their holes, and become convalescent, and increased and multiplied again more productively than ever. The great problem was, not how to kill the rats but how to annihilate them so effectually as to place the re-appearance of even one of them altogether out of the question. This was the problem and it was solved in the following manner:-

All the available inhabitants of the town were called to join in a great hunt. The rats were caught by every conceivable artifice; and, once taken, were instantly and ferociously smothered in onion; the corpses were then decently laid out on clean china dishes, and straightway [sic] eaten with vindictive relish by the people of Looe. Never was any invention for destroying rats so complete and so successful as this! Every man, woman, and child, who could eat, could swear to the expiration of all the rats they had eaten. The local returns of dead rats were not made by the bills of mortality, but by the bills of fare: it was getting rid of a nuisance by the unheard-of process of stomaching a nuisance! Day after day passed on, and rats disappeared by hundreds, never to return. What would their cunning and resolution avail them now?

They had resisted before, and could have resisted still, the ordinary force of dogs, ferrets, traps, sticks, stones, and guns, arrayed against them; but when to these engines of assault were added as auxiliaries, smothering with onions, scalding stew-pans, hungry mouths, sharp teeth, good digestions, and gastric juice, what could they do but give in? Swift and sure was the destruction that now overwhelmed them – everybody who wanted a dinner had a strong personal interest in hunting them down to the very last. In a short space of time the island was cleared of the usurpers. Cheeses remained entire: ricks rose uninjured. And this is the true story of how the people of Looe got rid of the rats!"

Despite the poetic licence this story is interesting for the reference to a shipwreck, which seems a plausible means for the rats to have arrived on the island, and mention of the farming that is known to have taken place there. A search of shipwreck records reveals that the *Rose* bound for Falmouth from Plymouth foundered on Looe Island 23rd January 1809 but according to the report in *The Times* on 30th January 1809 the crew and 33 passengers all lost their lives which does not accord with the Thomas Bond or Wilkie Collins text!

The diaries of Harriet Trelawny, the second wife of Lewis Trelawny, include tantalising references to the island as the following extracts from the entries reveal. These leather bound diaries are now in the Cornwall Record Office:

7th March 1874: Lewis [Trelawny] *and Alfred went to Looe Island . The sheep and lambs had been taken there.*

3rd January 1876: Lewis took possession of Looe Island

10th January 1876: Lewis and Gerald went to Looe Island and took some rabbits there.

26th January 1876: Lewis went again to Trelawne. They offered to build on the Island.

27th January 1876: Lewis and Gerald and I went to Looe Island to look for a site for the house.

18th November 1876: Lewis went out with all the keepers to catch rabbits on the Island. Dreadful disappointment as he only got 54.

18th November 1876: Lewis went to Looe Island and saw Cranford off and installed Nicholls and his wife there.

18th September 1879: We all went picnicking on the Island. It came on to rain and we had to sit in the house and came home very wet.

From a report of a case heard at Liskeard County Court 19th March 1894 we know that the island had, at that time, been leased for the past 15 years by a Potato Merchant, Ezra Joseph Neale of 24 Thomas Street, Bristol. His employee, Joseph Williams, a naval pensioner who lived on the island as caretaker with his wife claimed £5 damages because he alleged the leasee unlawfully entered and searched a dwelling house in his occupation and a further £2. 8s being the balance of a month's wages for dismissal without proper notice [his wages were 16s per week].

A detailed account of the dispute exists and it appears to have been a lively affair involving many threats. Joseph Williams became caretaker 18th September 1893 but by the following January Ezra Neale evidently suspected him of shooting rabbits and stealing a ferret together with some nets and cartridges. Neale arrived on the island at 7.30am on 22nd January 1894 with a 'gentleman friend from America'. Williams, the caretaker, carried Neale's luggage to his house and was then instructed to row to Looe for supplies. About 15 minutes later William T. Toms, the boatman, was instructed by Neale to take him back to Looe where they collected PC Holloway by prior arrangement and returned to the island. PC Holloway refused to search William's house without a warrant but Mrs Williams insisted they look for the missing items. A fracas developed on the beach when Williams returned from Looe and he was dismissed by Neale.

The court case revealed that Neale was something of a tyrant having hired and fired many caretakers during his tenancy (he could not remember how many but mentioned four in addition to Williams). The judge observed during the trial; that Neale seemed, in his own estimation, to be a sort of King and the "monarch of all he surveyed" which occasioned laughter in the court. It also emerged that he issued the caretaker with a rule-book containing forty 'urgent' rules plus all the ordinary rules. The third rule gives a clue to Neale's character: "Make no acquaintances with the Looe people, and have none of them on the island" and again: "Do not tell the Looe people that there are many rabbits here!"

The judge found for the plaintiff, stating that there was no justification for the charge of theft and awarding damages and costs against Neale. He did not allow the claim for wages considering that William's was a weekly employee but granted Mrs Williams £1.2s.6d for domestic work in Neale's House.

This was not the first instance of a charge of theft concerning the island. *The Cornish Times* reported in it's 11th August 1877 edition that Philip Hender, "who is supposed to be of weak intellect", was charged with stealing a painter, mast and sail (the property of W.L.S. Trelawny) from Looe Island the previous Monday evening. The report reveals that Sir William Trelawny kept two boats on the island in the charge of his employee James Henry Nicholls who resided there. It also confirms the presence of a boathouse on the island at that time.

Looe Island from the mainland (1890)

20th Century:

At the commencement of the 20th century the island was still in the hands of the Trelawne Estate of which the head at that time was Sir William Trelawny who inherited it when his father Sir John Trelawny died in 1885. In September 1912 it was let on a 21 year lease at £50 per year (expiring June 1933), to Henry St. John Dix Esq and a bill of sale c1920 (Lot 31) provides an interesting description of the property and buildings.

The Finance Act of 1910 (sometimes called Lloyd George's Domesday) required the Board of Inland Revenue to ascertain the site value of all land in England and Wales as at 30th April 1909. The National Archives, Kew, therefore holds a description of the island, and buildings thereon, prepared by the Valuation Office some time between 1910 and the completion of this huge [and expensive!] task in 1915. This confirms that the owner was Sir W.L.S. Trelawny Bart. of Trelawne, Duloe and the occupier one Dix who paid an annual rent of £50.00. The gross value was assessed at £1000 and the property described as:-

	Frontage	Depth	Ht.	Remarks
House:	33'9	16'6	18'	S & S. Plastered – Roof good
Bungalow: (old barn)	54'	19'6"	16'	S & S. Roof fair
Cottage	26'	24'	16'	S & S. Roof fair

Accommodation:

House: Dining – Kitchen – Scullery – 2 bedrooms - G.I. Covered passage with steps down to
Bungalow:- (Old Barn) – 4 bedrooms (small) – Store rooms – Wash House at rear.
(One floor) Cottage:- 3 Bedrooms – Kitchen – 2 small Pantries – Earth closet outdoors

A chronological listing of owners, residents and selected events is in Appendix 1.

LOOE ISLAND

A MOST UNIQUE, ATTRACTIVE AND VALUABLE PROPERTY, situated in Looe Bay, a short distance from the Mainland, with **Substantially Built RESIDENCE, Gardener's Cottage and Pasture Land,** extending in all to about

£2,175   2 1a.   or.   **8p.**

Let to HENRY ST. JOHN DIX, ESQRE, on a 21-years' Lease, expiring June, 1933, at a rental of

per £50 annum.

The HOUSE, which is well built of Stone and covered with Slate, together with a BUNGALOW COTTAGE adjoining, comprise together :—Entrance Hall ; wide partly glazed Corridor, used as a Lounge ; Dining Room ; Kitchen and good Domestic Offices ; six Bedrooms, etc. Pretty Gardens and Lawns surround the House.

At a convenient distance from the Main House there is a COTTAGE suitable for Keeper or Gardener with a good walled Vegetable and Fruit Garden, Orchard, etc.

The Residence, erected on the South Side of the Island, is well sheltered, the ground on the North of it rising to a height of about 200-feet above sea level. There are excellent private beaches.

Sale Catalogue, 16th September 1920

Chapter 6

THE CHAPEL

Little has been discovered about the pre-Christian history of the island but there is evidence of a Bronze Age burial on the adjacent mainland and it would be surprising if these people did not at least visit.

The religious history of St. George's starts with a persistent legend that Joseph of Arimathea [uncle of the Virgin Mary, being the younger brother of her father] took the infant Jesus with him to Cornwall on a voyage to trade in tin, and left him on the island whilst conducting his business. In his book *A Story of Looe Island*, published in 1966 and now difficult to find, F.E. Halliday expands upon this legend and even suggests that it inspired William Blake (1757–1827) to write his well known words:-

> *And did those feet in ancient time*
> *Walk upon England's mountains green?*
> *And was the Holy Lamb of God*
> *On England's pleasant pastures seen?*
> *And did the countenance Divine*
> *Shine forth upon our clouded hills?*
> *And was Jerusalem builded here*
> *Among these dark satanic mills?*

Whether or not you believe the legend, evidence survives that in 445 A.D., and probably very much earlier, tin was traded between Phoneicia and Cornwall. Furthermore, there is a 160 BC. reference to tin being mined in Cornwall and taken to an island called 'Ictis', "joined to the mainland at low tide". Unfortunately this description is equally relevant to the much larger St. Michael's Mount and also, at that time, a parcel of land surrounded by other lands was sometimes referred to as an 'island'. It should also be borne in mind that from 1144 the island was in the possession of the Benedictine abbey of Glastonbury and to claim that Jesus had visited would have enhanced their status. Glastonbury maintained Lammana, as the island was then called, for some 184 years. As far as can be determined the chapel on the island was built circa 1085 and was reached at low tide by means of a causeway that eventually became unsafe in the 12th century.

Anyone wishing to conduct further research on the above should seek copies of the following booklets [in secondhand bookshops as they are now out of print]:

1.   *Did our Lord Visit Britain as they say in Cornwall and Somerset?* by Rev. C.C. Dobson M.A. and published in 1936 with numerous subsequent reprints and revisions.
2.   *The Child Christ at Lammana* [2nd edition with additional notes] and *Christ in Cornwall* [1946], both by the Rev. H.A. Lewis, then vicar of St.Martins, Scilly Islands.

There is also a 1998 revision of a booklet *A Tale of Two Mediaeval Chapels in Lammana Parish* (Looe) by P.O. & D.V. Leggat dealing with the island and mainland chapels.

There is no mention of the island in Domesday but a document from Pope Lucius II in 1144 mentions 'Lamene' as a possession of Glastonbury and a subsequent document dated 1168 from his successor, Pope Alexander III, again refers to the possession but this time as 'Lamane'. This description embraces the island and the adjacent mainland and although chapels are not specifically mentioned it seems unlikely that Glastonbury would have maintained such a remote property unless it had a religious significance. The name in fact suggests the possibility of an even earlier religious settlement because the first element is probably derived from the Cornish 'Lan', a Celtic religious enclosure and it has been speculated that the second part of the name is a derogation of managh, 'monk'. Significantly the name does not mention St. Michael which is another indication of earlier Celtic religious activity.

In the 13th century Launceston Priory acquired the parish of Talland (on the mainland opposite the island) and found the value diminished because the monks of Glastonbury were entitled to privileges given by Portlooe Manor, including tithes. As early as 1144 the island had a cell of two Benedictine monks according to John Wallis, Vicar of Bodmin, in his 1847 book *The Cornwall Register*. A charter of c.1200, mentioned in a 1989 article by Lynette Olson and in *The Parochial History of Cornwall* by Mr Hals & Mr Tonkin (published 1838), appears to confirm these privileges. Roughly translated it says: "I Hastutus [alternative spellings are Hasculfus and Hastulus] son of Ionannes de Solenneio [alternative spelling Solenny] and Lord of Portlo, have granted and by the present charter confirmed to God and the church of the Blessed Virgin Mary of Glastonbury and to the convent of the same place the whole island of St. Michael of Lammana with all its appurtenances, both lands and tithes, which they hold from the ancient gift of my ancestor". Messrs Hals & Tonkin also refer somewhat enigmatically to a Roger Fitzwilliam "quitting his claims to lands of Lammana, which he held for life under the Abbey of Glastonbury, reserving the house his sister Mabil occupied". The dispute rumbled on however and in 1289 the then Abbot of Glastonbury demised the rights in the chapel of Lammana to Walter de Treverbyn, Lord of the Manor of Portlooe. The Prior of Launceston continued to claim however that the rights to the tithes belonged to the priory's church at Talland and the matter went to court at Westminster. The case was soon adjourned so that the sheriff of Cornwall could bring to Westminster twelve unbiased men competent to testify the facts in the matter. This eventually took place in October 1290 and the discovery of a record of their evidence by Keith Hamylton Jones in 1983 confirms that the chapel on the island, dedicated to St. Michael the Archangel, pre-dates the chapel on the mainland. This, of course, is in Latin but what the twelve jurors said was that "Lammana is a sea girt island in which a certain chapel of Saint Michael used to be kept up where the abbots of Glastonbury, time out of mind, had monks celebrating Divine Service. And, because in days of old many of those people who through devotion would have wanted to visit the said chapel on Saint Michael's Day often lost their lives in the stormy sea a certain chapel of Saint Michael was constructed on the coast opposite the said island." They went on to confirm that the abbots of Glastonbury had always been in receipt of the tithes thus dismissing the claims of Launceston priory. The value of the tithes was assessed at 100 shillings per annum.

In passing it is interesting to note that in his book *A History of Cornwall* published in 1838, Gilbert writes of the mainland chapel:-

"I measured this chapel on the 13th April 1815 and found it, within the walls, forty-seven feet long by twenty-four wide. About three or four hundred yards to the eastward of the chapel are the remains of some ancient building, perhaps that in which the monks dwelt. The remains of the eastern end wall thereof, at present eight or ten feet high, have two very narrow windows or openings, still in being. The situation of this chapel and house is very pleasant; they lie in a sort of natural amphitheatre, sheltered from the north winds by high land."

In a 1985 article, W.M.M. Picken speculates that the motivation for the monks to build a chapel on the mainland (also dedicated to St. Michael the Archangel) may have had more to do with their convenience than concern for pilgrims! The elevated situation could also be an indication that a beacon light was maintained there to assist navigation. Be that as it may however, the court case confirms beyond doubt that the first chapel was on the summit of "the island of St. Michael of Lammana" as it was then called.

To view the mainland chapel simply walk to the western end of the road at Hannafore Point and follow the signed footpath uphill, first pausing to see the remains of a 13th century monastic building in the hedge between the last house on the right (Monk's House) and the field.

A list of 'Chaplains of Lamana on Looe Island' prepared by a past vicar of Talland church, the Revd. Timberlake, can still be seen on an inscribed slate dated 1942 in the Sanctuary window of the church and reads as follows:

1200	Prior Helyas	
1285	Andrew	
1329	William de Trewidel	Priest
1343	Adam Brian	Deacon
1348	John Doygnel	Priest
1352	Richard Abeham	Priest
1381	John Strangelonde	Cantor
1388	Nicholas Walronde	
1405	John Lyne	
1433	Robert Symon	

1456　John Wylt
1457　John Tauton
　......　George
1503　Walter Kyndon M.A.
1513　John Cocke
　......　John Cole　　　　　　Cantor
1528　David Hengsley
1537　Robert Swymmer

It seems likely that the chapel on the summit of the island fell into disuse following the suppression of Chantries in 1547. An assessment of the assets by Henry VIII's successor, Edward VI in 1548 revealed that the island chantry chapel had no valuables and services were infrequent. The mainland chapel had just 6oz of plate and jewels. The only clue we have to the appearance of the chapel is from a Tudor map of the coast between Fowey and Looe that includes a drawing of a rectangular chapel with a pitch roof on the island. This map is now in the British Museum. In the Victorian era there are references to visible remains and today two carved pieces of stone remain in a grassy hollow near the summit. At the time of writing there is no evidence of the island chapel site having ever been excavated apart from the reported discovery of the skeleton of a tall man here a long time ago.

It is interesting to note that a chapel that survives on a headland at St. Ives on the Atlantic coast of Cornwall closely resembles the illustration on the Tudor map in the British Library. Much closer to the island the shell of a small chapel survives at Rame head.

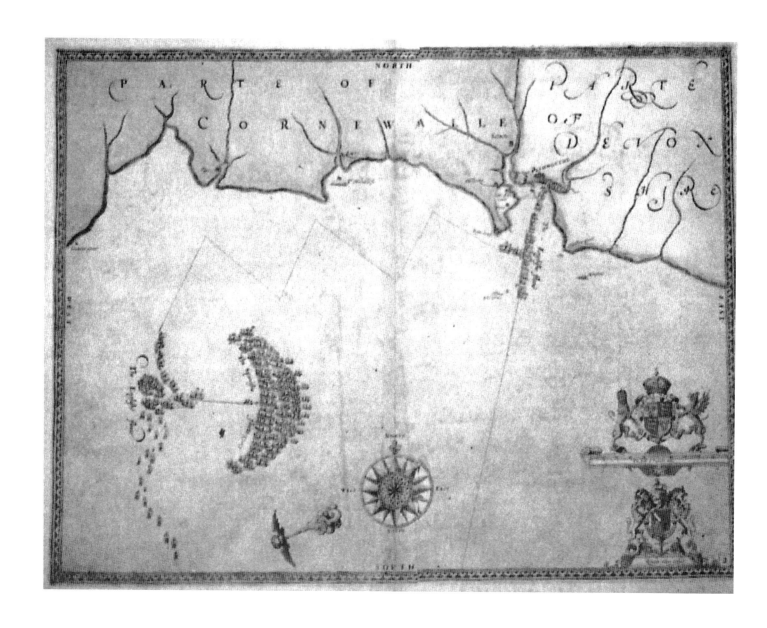

The Spanish Armada forms a defensive crescent south of the island.

Chapter 7

ENGLAND THREATENED

The Spanish Armada:
The sight of the Spanish Armada making its way up the Channel in July 1588, after an unseasonably rough crossing from Spain, was an awesome spectacle viewed with apprehension from the coast of Cornwall and beacons flashed news of the threat across the country.

As darkness fell on the night of the 29th July the English ships were to leeward of the Armada i.e. between the Spanish fleet and the shore, but unseen they manoeuvred some 54 ships behind the Armada on which they bore down with the prevailing wind the next morning. Although heavily outnumbered (the Armada comprised 130 vessels) this gave them an advantage and the Spanish fleet changed its formation to a huge defensive crescent of which many accounts have survived. A series of contemporary maps depicting the engagement of the two fleets clearly show that the defensive crescent was formed to the south of the island. It is assumed, therefore, that anyone standing on the summit of the island would have seen both fleets which must have been both impressive and alarming.

The Armada off Looe Island in 1588
pursued by the English fleet

47

The discovery of two cannon balls buried on the main beach some years ago inevitably gave rise to speculation that they may be connected with this momentous event. However, there is no reference to action close to the island in contemporary accounts and it seems more likely that they were used in a skirmish with Turkish or other pirates who sometimes raided Looe in the past.

For the record there were three indecisive engagements with the Spanish over a period of several days off Plymouth, Portland Bill and the Isle of Wight before the Armada anchored near Calais on the 6th August. The English fleet was then reinforced by ships diverted from the blockade of the Netherlands and a decision made to sail fire ships into the defensive crescent of the Spanish fleet. Although the Spanish anticipated this tactic it proved successful and the English secured victory.

World War II:
In modern times the island became briefly, and rather bizarrely, involved in WWII when an aerial mine was dropped by a German aircraft at 7pm on Sunday, 1st December 1940. A report from Superintendent Sleeman, who investigated for the police, states "a terrific explosion was heard on Looe Island, off Looe". Investigation revealed a crater 30ft wide by 12ft deep near the summit, damage to two houses but no casualties as the island was uninhabited. Independent reports say windows were broken on the mainland nearly a mile away. Supt. Sleeman went on to speculate that the bomb was a parachute mine as no engine noise from an aeroplane was heard. In a second report the same day he advised that a 'Paramine' cap was found on the foreshore of Looe island bearing the stencil marking L.D662 in red thus confirming that a parachute mine caused the explosion. The supposition is that the raider mistook the island for a vessel in the misty gloom of evening and the *Cornish Times* suggested that the BBC newsreader Alvar Liddell could taunt William Joyce (who broadcast propaganda on behalf of the Nazi regime) with "What happened to the raider who tried to sink HMS St. George?"! For the record, William Joyce, who was nick-named Lord Haw-Haw in Britain, was executed for treason after the war because he held a British passport when he first began his broadcasts from Germany. A piece of the silk cord that connected the parachute to the mine was recovered from the scene by a Mr Hooper and is now in the Old Guildhall Museum, Looe.

In November 2004, following a severe storm, wreckage from a B17 Flying Fortress was recovered from the sea just off Seaton, and within sight of the island, including an engine complete with propeller. The aircraft had been badly damaged by enemy fire and was off course with little fuel. The pilot, 21 year old Lieutenant Robert J. Denissen, waited until his crew had bailed out over land and then moments before the aircraft hit the sea he too parachuted to safety. Lt. Denissen was recovered from the sea by a couple in a rowing boat and although he suffered severe hypothermia he lived into his eighties. His widow has been informed of the discovery of the B17 and it is hoped that the engine recovered will be displayed in Old Guildhall Museum, Looe.

The B17 propellor with Looe Island in the background

Chapter 8

SHIPS & THE SEA

The rugged coast of Cornwall has claimed many victims, especially in the days of sail, and inevitably some have been associated with the island or occurred nearby.

In January 1809 *The Times* reported the loss of thirty-three passengers and crew when the packet *Rose*, bound for Falmouth from Plymouth, was wrecked on the island. On the same day another vessel, believed to be Dutch, was reported to have sunk in Mount's Bay with the loss of all aboard so one imagines the conditions were difficult that day.

Ships driven ashore during the 18th century in particular frequently fell prey to the 'wreckers' who operated on the Cornish coast stripping vessels of cargo and material for profit. Within sight of the island this practice was pursued and in March 1750 the *Sherborne Mercury* newspaper reported that the *Endeavor*, en route from Exeter to Cadiz,

The *St. Pierre* aground in 1906. Looe Island in the background

was stranded at Downderry and Customs officers had to resort to firing shots to drive off wreckers! In another incident at Looe not long after, hordes of local people descended on a stranded vessel and even the guards appointed by the Customs officers joined in the looting! And not all shipwrecks were accidents! All round the coast of Cornwall people engaged in 'wrecking' i.e. salvaging cargoes and material from vessels that foundered and some were not above engineering disasters by luring ships ashore with false navigation beacons.

The offer of a one guinea reward in the *West Briton* newspaper for 5th January 1816 reveals another tragedy and who occupied the island at the time. The advertisement read:-

> "Whereas the body of Benjamin Christopher, who was drowned on the 16th December 1815, near Plymouth breakwater has not yet been discovered, it is hoped that whoever may find the body will give immediate information to his mother, Mrs Elizabeth Hooper, of Looe Island, who will give the above reward [one guinea], and take charge of the body.
>
> He was about 30 years old, 5ft 10 inches high, well made – fair complexion – very light hair, had on a blue jacket and trowsers – blue frock, light worsted stockings and a yellow silk hankerchief [sic].
>
> Benjamin Christopher, who lived with his mother on Looe Island, had left there for Plymouth in an open boat with lobsters."

In 1838 a winter gale blew the brig *Bellisima* onto the rocks to the seaward of the island. The vessel broke-up but 13 lives were saved by a brave individual who entered the rough sea and managed to get a line aboard the brig.

An especially high profile fatality was Dr. Harty and his boatman in September 1894. They were sailing in his boat from Looe to Polperro but never arrived and were last seen alive by Thomas Toms, a Looe fisherman, about 200 to 300 yards west of the island. At the inquest, which followed the recovery of the bodies, it emerged that Dr Harty had previously been warned that his craft carried too much sail to be safe at sea! His popularity in the area can be gauged from a report in *The Cornish Times* for 22nd September 1894 stating that over 2,000 people attended his funeral at St. Martins-by-Looe.

Island life is dominated by the sea with tides and waves not only determining when access is possible but also bringing surprises, some pleasant and some decidedly otherwise. A rather splendid china owl washed up on the beach in pristine condition was a welcome find for the Atkins sisters but on another occasion the sea brought them a body that turned out to be an old lady they knew! Shipwrecked mariners are another fact of island life and one in particular was fortunate to be rescued. His speedboat had foundered on the rocks, leaving him clinging to a buoyancy cushion in a rough sea. When his plight was spotted, 'Attie' and a visitor launched the island dinghy and managed to rescue him cold, shaken and with no harm that a change of clothes and hot tea could not remedy.

As recently as January 2002, a Russian cargo vessel ran aground within view of the Island at Whitsand Bay shedding a huge amount of timber, much to the benefit of local D.I.Y. enthusiasts!

Looe Island Whale: A report in the *Cornish Times* 27th December 1929:-

"When daylight broke on Sunday morning the local coastguards noticed a huge object lying on the beach on Looe Island which, on investigation, proved to be the carcase of a large Porgual whale. Measurements were taken and it was found that the monster was 53'. 8 inches from nose to tip of tail, and 36' around its thickest part
Much interest was taken in the unusual visitant, people going out in boats to examine the carcase. The mammal, judging by its appearance, had not been dead long, and close examination could be made in comfort.
The disposal of the remains will be no small problem as there must be many tons of carcass to remove, and, judging by a similar experience some years ago when a much smaller specimen was washed ashore at Looe beach, the odour will become somewhat obnoxious unless a quick means of removal is found.
Fortunately the island is about a mile from Looe, and the ozone should be filtered by the time it reached the twin towns.
A portion of the whale, weighing about one hundred weight, was despatched yesterday by rail to the British Museum. Its presence on Liskeard Station was self-evident.".

A 1929 photograph of the stranded whale survives and is interesting because a horse and rider can be seen on the skyline. How did they get there, one wonders?!

Select list of shipwrecks: See Appendix 2

Chapter 9

FREE TRADERS

In the 18th & 19th centuries smuggling was a major industry in Cornwall despite the efforts of the understaffed revenue authorities and harsh penalties for convicted offenders. The high duties imposed on a variety of luxury goods imported from Europe by successive British governments made smuggling very profitable for anyone prepared to face little more risk than most people at the time encountered in their everyday struggle to earn a living.

Brandy, gin, tea and tobacco were all readily available across the Channel at considerably lower prices than they were in England. Because the Channel Islands were exempt from taxes imposed by a British parliament, they became the main centre for the supply of goods. Cornwall's proximity to the merchants of St Peter Port on Guernsey ensured that the trade in contraband goods was particularly active. At one time there were some 2,000 coopers on Guernsey alone making tubs for spirits to be smuggled to England!

Smuggling boat with tubs slung for sinking

Smugglers used several ploys for concealing the contraband from the preventive officers before running it ashore. A common and ingenious method involved the use of sinking stones, one of which can be seen (right) by visitors to the island at Jetty Cottage. Tubs being smuggled were often strung together along the side of the craft like a string of pearls and weighted with 'sinking stones' (hence there is a hole through the stone for the rope). The smugglers could then drop them overboard, especially if surprised by a Revenue cutter, carefully noting their position by reference to landmarks and then return when the coast was clear to retrieve them. Since the tubs were buoyant it was easy to catch hold of the rope along which they were strung using special grapnels called 'creepers'.

The island was an ideal staging post for landing and concealing goods until it was safe to ferry them to the mainland. The contraband included small casks of spirits known as 'tubs', tea, silk stockings and other goods subject to a high duty. In 1816 for example the *West Briton & Cornwall Advertiser* newspaper reported that the cargo of a French vessel, that had to be assisted into Looe harbour after nearly running aground, included twelve toy horses in which were concealed some 51 pairs of silk stockings and nine silk shawls. The *West Briton* newspaper for 15th May 1818 carried a report; "On Saturday last, the preventive boats from Polperro and Wrinkle, took up a raft of contraband spirits, near Looe Island, containing 106 ankers [1 anker = 8 gallons], which they lodged in the excise warehouse at Looe." Metal brackets still to be seen in the precipitous western cliffs of the island are thought to have been installed to facilitate hauling contraband from sea level.

Tea was one favoured smuggled commodity but spirits were also a popular cargo and a late 18th century estimate is that half the spirits consumed in the kingdom had no duty paid on them. Because Guernsey was the main source of much of the Cornish contraband and had a particularly well established smuggling trade with Polperro along the coast, it is probable that some cargoes would have been landed on the island to supplement the income of the inhabitants at the time.

With the cessation of hostilities with France in 1815, smuggling entered a second phase, called the 'scientific period' by Henry Shore in *Smuggling Days and Smuggling Ways,* published in 1892. There were changes on both sides of the trade; more men, freed from the armed forces, were recruited into peace keeping forces in the

Channel. Faced with added vigilance, the smugglers adapted their vessels to escape or delay detection of illegal cargoes.

In 1816, Laws for the Prevention of Smuggling were enacted and regulations set in place to prevent gatherings of three or more, possibly armed, from being involved in 'rescuing' goods. If convicted, transgressors might face the death penalty. Similar penalties were intended to prevent the wearing of masks or blackened faces whilst engaged on handling illegal imports.

Roscoff emerged as a new port or 'entrepot' for supplies, although this was to prove dangerous since there were spies there who informed the authorities of the dispatch of cargoes together with their destinations. The *Daniel & William* was reported, on one occasion, in 1833, as leaving the port with a cargo for Looe Island "with 130 tubs". The ship was active in the Looe area in the 1830s and appears in Wisdom Penaluna's account (see Appendix 3) of local activities directly linked to Amram Hooper. As a means of disguise, the vessel carried two sets of sails, one white, one tanned. She was later caught and, in accordance with regulations, sawn into three parts.

There were three distinct stages in the smuggling process: bringing the goods over, landing them and, finally, running them inland. The island was ideally placed for vigilance at each stage of the operations and any information given could be counteracted by sharp eyes and a secure hiding place.

Given the illicit nature of the trade it is hardly surprising that records of smuggling activity tend to be sketchy at best but enough is known to leave us in no doubt that the island witnessed a very brisk trade in years gone by. Indeed a watch-house was introduced in the early 19th century to accommodate an Excise Officer and the 1841 census records that it was then James Galway aged 40 and Robert Galway aged 15 (presumably his son). By the time of the 1851 census John Connor, Commissioned Boatman, attached to Looe Coastguard was at the

'Coastguard Watch House' on the island. Most unfortunately, the records of the Customs & Excise at Fowey were deliberately destroyed in 1878, thus depriving us of a valuable source of information. Nevertheless, by diligently researching other sources, some of the story of this fascinating aspect of the island's past has been pieced together by Barbara Birchwood-Harper.

Prior to 1815, the old established 'Free Trading' which had been carried on for centuries between England and the continent was conducted with what Henry Shore calls "a freedom from interruption" He gives an account which he claims typifies the way in which the trade was carried on in Cornwall. A traveller, a town dweller, arrived on a beach as a cargo of smuggled goods was being landed. He observed the delivery ship laying offshore and a number of small boats ferrying goods back to the shore where a large and rowdy crowd applied themselves to the distribution (and sampling!) of the goods. Appalled by the scene, the stranger, having enquired about the whereabouts of the local magistrate and been told he was about eight miles away, then asked if there was a local clergyman, only to be told: "That's he, sir, yonder, with the lanthorn".

Shore's *The Old Smugglers Tale* in 1899, mentions Looe Island as the destination for a cargo of what the smuggler, from Cawsand, called 'sperrits' (brandy). The beach, which would have been ideal for landings, faces the shore, the rest of the Island having jagged rocks. It would have been a brave or foolhardy man who brought a vessel too close to the south or west coast of the island.

Many strange tales abound: a black man supposedly murdered, a skeleton with long fingers, a ghost which manifests in a blue light. However, in terms of a venue for smuggling it was ideally situated and ghostly tales would keep snoopers away.

No account of the smugglers of Looe Island would be complete without mentioning Thomas Fletcher, an Irishman who came to Looe as a coastguard in the 1830s. He married a local woman, raised a large family and absconded from the coastguard service to join the smugglers. A tradition in the Fletcher family is that Thomas himself was caught smuggling and sent to London for trial, but as he continued to live in Looe, it may well be just a myth.

Thomas Fletcher (1813-1896)

57

This example of a coastguard changing sides was not unique in Looe; Henry Shore relates that no fewer than three chief officers in succession were dismissed for collusion. Looe is a small community and as the coastguards lived in the same streets as the smugglers, a certain amount of sympathy, envy, fear and pressure was bound to result in such situations occurring.

There is a large picture in the Council chamber in the Guildhall in Looe entitled 'The arrest of the Smuggler' which is said to depict Fletcher despite being dated 1820, well before his arrival in the town.

Thomas Fletcher was given one of the famous walking funerals to his last resting place in Schlerder Abbey above Talland bay.

Smugglers entering Looe Harbour at night?

Chapter 10

THE MEWSTONE CONNECTION

The island has been inhabited at least since the latter half of the 18th century when it was occupied by the Finn family whose mysterious link with the Mewstone, an uninhabited island off Wembury, near Plymouth, is referred to by the Rev. Stebbing Shaw in 1788 (see Chapter 5, page 30).

Shaw refers to the story of a man who had been banished to the Mewstone in 1774 for a term of seven years, "whose name is Finn, and by his own industrious cultivation... reaps a comfortable subsistence [on Looe Island]."

The crime for which Finn was punished was obviously not a capital offence since 18th century laws were harsh and even petty crimes attracted the death penalty. More likely it was one of nuisance to his neighbours, who may have made representations to the local magistrate to have him removed. In 1781 the 'Mewstone Man' moved to Looe Island with his wife, having served his sentence.

The recent discovery by local Looe historian Barbara Birchwood-Harper of a Bible (right) belonging to the Finn and Hooper families has shed some light on the occupants of the island at the end of the 18th century. Inside the front cover is an almost indecipherable entry that includes the words 'George Finn his name'.

Inside the back cover is the following:
George Finn.......................
When this you see, Remember me
And this bear in your mind   *Remember thy Creator*
Let all the world say what they will,
Speak of me as you find   *Always*
George Finn.

A line further down the page, after the entry of the 1800 baptism, is as follows:
John Finn departed this life December 25th and in the year of our Lord God 1800 aged 77 years

This entry has been confirmed by the entry of his burial on the aforementioned date, at Morval Church. Records of two further burials at Morval are of members of the Finn family where the abode is given as Looe Island. Elizabeth Finn aged 86, was buried on 5th November 1818 and John Finn aged 75 was buried on 14th August 1835.

These details and the George Finn entries in the Finn/Hooper Bible point to the fact that this family is one and the same as the Finn family whose details are recorded in the parish registers of Stoke Damerel in Plymouth (the shadow of the Mewstone again?).

Baptism of John Finn, son of John and Elizabeth Finn, 9th November 1760 (matching the 1835 burial details)

The tantalising question is why the Finn and Hooper details appear together in the same Bible. Both families were obviously on Looe Island at the same time.

Thomas Bond, in his history of East and West Looe, published in 1823, confirms that the "Finn family have inhabited the Island for the past 40 years", giving a possible date of 1783 which, with approximations, would tie in with the end of the seven year sentence imposed in 1774.

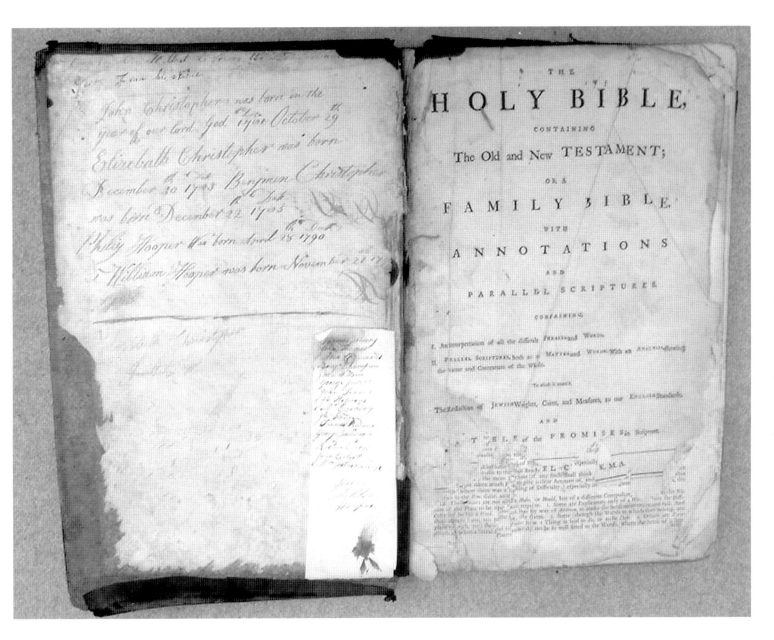

John Christopher was born in the
year of our Lord God 1781 October 29th
Elizabeth Christopher was born
December 30 1783 Benjamin Christopher
was born December 22 1785
Philip Hooper was born April 28 1790
William Hooper was born November 21 17—

THE

HOLY BIBLE,

CONTAINING

The Old and New TESTAMENT;

OR A

FAMILY BIBLE,

WITH

ANNOTATIONS

AND

PARALLEL SCRIPTURES

Also, the evidence from the family Bible kept by the Finns and Elizabeth Hooper, suggests that the Finn family who lived on the island and were subsequently buried at Morval could well be the Finn family recorded in Stoke Damerel in the 1760s (see page 60 for details).

This family (John Finn, baptised in 1760, and George Finn, baptised 1763, both sons of John and Elizabeth Finn) seems to fit with the Finn details from the Morval registers. There is no recorded burial for George Finn 'of Looe Island' but a later burial at Morval, of a George Finn 'of Devonport' is a possibility despite the fact that the age at death does not fit with George baptised in 1763.

Barbara Birchwood-Harper was at the Cornwall Records Office, looking through the baptism register for Talland church, when she came upon an unusual entry:

> *Amram and Jochabed, the son and daughter of Anthony Hooper of Looe Island were baptised on June 25th 1800. The former (Amram) 4years (21/11) and Jochabed 9 years 28/4 last.*

> *Godparents:-.*
> *Mary Kendall   Rev'd William Hocken*
> *Amelia Kendall   George Bewett esq*
> *Margaret Hart   John Penrose esq*
> *   William Beard*
> *signed C. Kendall vicar*

Their mother's name was not given, but later investigations and a copy of her will dated 1843 introduced Elizabeth Hooper as mother of Jochabed and Amram.

Barbara made a note of the entry, unaware what a colourful pair they would turn out to be in the history of smuggling in Looe.

The names themselves, are intriguing; they indicate parents who knew their Bible. The names appear in Exodus chapter 6 verse 20:

"And Amram took him Jochebed his father's sister to wife; and she bore him Aaron and Moses: and the years of the life of Amram were an hundred and thirty seven years."

20 And [f] Amram took him Jochebed his [21] father's fifter to wife; and fhe bare him Aaron and Mofes: and the years of the life of Amram *were* an hundred and thirty and feven years.

The Rev. Timberlake, one time incumbent at Talland church, made the following comments concerning the details of the christening entry:-

"The fullness of the entry is quite unique for the period, and the inclusion of names of Godparents of the latter, all with the possible exception of William Beard, who could be 'Marine of West Looe', are certainly country gentry - Kendalls of Polsu inter-married with the Hext of Lanlivery. Revd W. Hocken (snr) was a rector of Lanteglos-by-Fowey from 1805, his son or grandson, vicar of Talland 1844-1858."

The Finn/Hooper Bible, which has the same details of the baptism entered by the vicar's hand, also poses intriguing mysteries. The first of these being that the births of Amram and Jochabed were recorded in the traditional manner, but that the original names they were given were Philly and William (the dates of their births match those given at baptism). The entries are as follows:-

Philly Hooper 28th April 1790

William Hooper born November 21st 1795

These dates are the dates on which Amram and Jochabed were born! Perhaps this explains why the children's mother was absent from the christening ceremony. Did she disapprove of the baptismal names?

Little is known about the children's father, Anthony Hooper, apart from his appearance at the christening, and that he married Elizabeth Christopher, a widow, at St George's, Stonehouse (Plymouth) on 15th September 1789. He may have been the Anthony Justy Hooper born in Morval in 1746.

Elizabeth, baptised 29th March 1759, was the daughter of John and Elizabeth Vening who were married in Abbotskerswell, Devon, in 1752.

Elizabeth had previously been married to Benjamin Christopher by whom she had three children. An entry of October 30th 1777 records the marriage of Elizabeth Vening to Benjamin Christopher of *HMS Boyne*.

The entries in the family Bible, give the following birth dates of their three children:
John Christopher born October 29th 1781
Elizabeth Christopher born December 30th 1783
Benjamin Christopher born December 22nd 1785

Elizabeth was baptised on 11th January 1784; John was baptised 5th March 1787 in Pelynt (was this a second son of this name? There seems no reason for the gap between a birth in 1781 and a baptism in 1787). Benjamin was baptised 28th August 1789 at Talland.

Both Elizabeth and John are mentioned in their mother's will, drawn up in 1829, but Benjamin is believed to have been lost at sea.

In the *West Briton*, of 5th January 1816, there is a promise of a reward of one guinea, from "Mrs Elizabeth Hooper of Looe Island" to anyone finding the body of her 30-year-old son, Benjamin Christopher, who was drowned on 16th December 1815 near Plymouth breakwater. The description she gave of him appears in chapter 8.

Whereas the history of smuggling in Polperro is well documented, information about smuggling activities in Looe is limited. By its very nature, the trade was a secretive one and if, as we believe, Amram and Jocabed were heavily involved with it, they would have been very guarded about their family details.

One of the stories about Looe Island is the tale of 'Black Joan and Fyn', possibly brother and sister, who had supposedly lived on Looe Island at some period and had been formidable smugglers. Naturally, being aware of the fact that smugglers adopted nicknames and that stealth, lies and cunning were the tools of their trade, Barbara Birchwood-Harper investigated the possibility of the two couples being one and the same. She consulted authors who had tackled the subject. Sabine Baring-Gould had some information about Joan and Fyn: they were, reputedly, the children of an outlaw who had lived on the Mewstone off Plymouth. On Fyn's death, they moved to Looe Island. But, if Anthony Hooper was living on Looe Island when the children were born and baptised, where does the Mewstone story fit in?

The Mewstone
Photo by John Such/Scan Air,
courtesy of the National Trust

Confusingly, the Rev. Shaw's account in 1788 says the daughter of the man on the Mewstone was a widow at that time, her husband having lately drowned and leaving three children. It has even been suggested that she was Elizabeth Christopher who later became Elizabeth Hooper.

Amram and Jochabed were undoubtedly the brother and sister known as 'Fyn and Black Joan'. For one thing, by the time Amram's smuggling career was at its height in the 1820s, the elder Finns were dead.

Jochabed was described by local author Elizabeth Steed Shapcott, writing in the 1920s having obtained the information from one of Jochabed's contemporaries: "The last of the old smugglers to live on the island were a brother and sister, Amram and Jochabed… They were a very strange couple, the woman far more like a man."

A further description of Jochabed says: "She was more like a man. She dressed like one, rowed a boat, smoked a pipe and could use her fists when occasion required. She wore a man's hat, a blue knitfrock and boots; the only women's thing about her was a skirt but this was always rolled up and fastened above her knees."

The 1793 account by a visitor, (see chapter 5, page 32) concerning the identities of the inhabitants, is vague although the 'old man of 70' was probably Finn. The matter of some of the children being grandchildren could well have been an assumption.

It is possible that Elizabeth Christopher (née Vening) and her children living in the Looe area, may have been befriended by the Finn family, then on the island, when she married Anthony Hooper, given that John Finn was getting on in years. The whole family joined them in tilling the soil of the island and harvesting the profitable harvest from the sea (via Guernsey!).

Many court records perished in the WWII bombing of Plymouth, and details of 'Mewstone Man's' crime in 1774 have not survived. We are left with a few facts, some written proof of rites of passage and much conjecture from both visitors and local people. One day, perhaps, we may find the other pieces of this intriguing jigsaw puzzle.

Amram's Descendants

Amram Hooper had married a local girl, Philippa Medland, at Talland in 1823. Their first son Benjamin was baptised there on 25th March 1823 but died two years later. The couple's next son, also called Benjamin, was baptised on 29th April 1827 at St. Martins church, East Looe. A daughter, Matilda, was baptised on 15th May 1825. Three more daughters were born to the couple: Elizabeth, baptised on 14th June 1829, Susannah Philippa, baptised on 9th May 1836 and Ellen, baptised on February 11th 1837, all at St. Martin's.

The 1841 census records that Amram, Philippa and their children were living in East Looe. All, that is, except Susannah who was living in West Looe with her aunt, Jochabed, who had married a man called Thomas Broad from St Ive.

Another name linked with Amram Hooper's smuggling activities is that of 'Island Til' or 'Island Lil'. In 1841 a lady called Matilda Bartlett was living on the island with the Hooper household, but whether 'Island Lil' or 'Til' was this Matilda or Amram's daughter is anyone's guess.

Some notes in an archive at the Old Guildhall in East Looe record that 'the smuggler', presumably Amram Hooper, moved off the island and married 'a lady of Looe'. According to the writer, Amram's children were not involved in smuggling nor were they aware of his activities. The same source records that Jochabed returned to the mainland, married and lived a quiet and industrious life.

A further biographical piece describes 'the smuggler' as "most remarkable, evidently educated far above his surroundings, had great personality and charm, clever, resourceful, a born leader and his associates revered him. He was, however, a most silent man, no one knew where he came from and there were many tales and rumours about him".

It was said his family were superior people and were punished for some state offence. He was in a college of learning at the time and his whole career was wrecked. What he did was done in a spirit of revenge against the law of the land, more than for the profit it bought him. A local fisherman whom he employed to go out fishing with him said, when asked by his wife what they talked about, "his words were few, but pure silver every one of 'em".

As to who the mystery man really was, the truth may never be discovered.

Chapter 11

CAVES & TREASURE

The Mystery of the Lost Caverns

Henry Shore claimed that the "cave dwellings wherein the trusty Hamram and his daughter imprisoned the spirits entrusted to their care" were eventually discovered, one accidentally and one by a process known in the profession as 'pricking' - probing the ground with long pointed rods. If this is true, however, the knowledge appears to have been lost and the location of all but one of the caves remains a mystery to this day. It is interesting to note that Shore's observations came not long after a similar report in the *Cornish Times* (15th September 1900). Tantalisingly, this promised a "specially written and detailed description of these remarkable discoveries" in the next issue but no such report appeared. If the original report is to be believed, the nature of the caverns is surprising and the report is therefore reproduced below in full for readers to form their own judgement:

REMARKABLE DISCOVERIES AT LOOE ISLAND

Two years ago two gentlemen, spending their holidays at Looe, were struck by an article in the *Cornish Times* which, among other interesting matter, alluded to the smuggling formerly carried out at the island and the cave said to be thereon, the locality of which was unknown to any person in existence.

Having nothing to occupy their time, these gentlemen (Messrs R. Lawson, of the Inner Temple, and F.A. Somers, F.S.A.) resolved to investigate the matter. The kind consent and cordial assistance of the proprietor (Sir William Trelawny) were obtained, and a year ago the work was commenced in earnest, but in great secrecy.

The cave was soon found, and shortly after an adjoining one, which, from its curious resemblance to the celebrated Etruscan caves at Clusia in central Italy, led the investigators to suspect that they had accidentally stumbled on a discovery unknown even to the old smugglers themselves.

This season it was determined to make further excavations, and most remarkable results have been obtained.

At a distance of about 18ft below the surface, St. George's Island is nothing but an extensive ramification of caves. Everything points to the fact that these were originally above ground, and that at some later date a mass of ground was superimposed, most probably by some natural agency. The term 'cave' does not really apply, as many of the larger ones – and there are scores – are built of brick, similar to that used on the Hannafore Estate and probably obtained from the same source.

They are evidently very ancient, probably prehistoric, and several have collapsed. The style of 'architecture' is that of very early pre-maesopelagic or Etruscan. One or two very interesting finds have been made, but nothing in the shape of human remains.

The cemetery on the island was, in all probability, made by the monks at a very much later period.

Further important developments are expected, and it is hoped that before the end of the month, by kind permission of Mr A.E. Preston, all the excavations will be thrown open to the public, when a small charge will be made for the Looe Lifeboat and District Nurse Funds.

Caves on the west side of Looe Island

While it is common knowledge that smuggling was once rife in Cornwall, the visitor may be surprised to learn that as recently as 1979 large quantities of cannabis from North Africa were being smuggled ashore at Talland Bay, just two miles west of St. George's Island. The gang, who used a converted trawler called *Guiding Lights*, was eventually caught one night in September 1979 bringing ashore some 2.5 tons of cannabis and subsequently 13 men were convicted for the offence in London.

Treasure!

If smuggled goods could be secreted on the island so could treasure and there have been many local stories of hidden caches and even a tunnel to the mainland at Hannafore. No doubt such convenient access to and from the mainland would have been a boon to smugglers but the briefest consideration of the logistics of such an excavation, even with today's technology, suggests this legend is no more than romantic fiction.

Treasure, or even perhaps the remains of some smuggled goods, is a more realistic possibility so there was considerable excitement when, some years ago, the Atkins sisters received an authentically old-looking treasure map from a clergyman in Cumbria who stated it had been in his family for several generations. At the time they were too busy to investigate beyond experimenting with dousing which, to their astonishment, brought a strong reaction for both of them at the point marked 'X' on the map. Some years later dousing produced the same reaction and at this point an island volunteer stepped in to excavate the area but sadly his efforts were not rewarded although dowsing continued to bring a powerful reaction. More recently, a geophysical survey of the island suggests there is a large rock buried deep at the point in question but, alas, no horde of gold coins.

Surveys with metal detectors have also been made but the only finds have been a Victorian penny and two cannon balls

Chapter 12

THINGS THAT GO BUMP IN THE NIGHT!

Cornwall abounds with ghost stories so it is not surprising to learn that St. George's has its own legends. One such, based upon information from a local lady of 92 who claimed she could well remember the events of 87 years ago, was recounted by local author, Elizabeth Shapcott in 1928:

"Of course the island was haunted; that was well known. One ghost was that of a black man, evidently killed in a fight, as when he was seen blood was always streaming from his face – but I have no particulars of this tale.

My old lady informant was a needlewoman and dressmaker, and it was usual then for dressmakers and tailors to go to the houses of their customers and do the required work there, staying perhaps a week or a fortnight at a time. Somewhere about 1850 a farmer and his wife ------ by name [William and Jane Vague aged 30 and 23 respectively were there for the 1851 census] occupied the island. They were a young couple with two small children. Mrs ------ besides being a customer, was also a friend of the old lady, and about that date the latter went to the island to do some sewing. It was May month, the weather was fine, and quite a treat to be away from the mainland. Mr ------ had some business to do in the country beyond Looe, and took the opportunity of doing it while the old lady was in his home for as he was unable to leave until the latter part of the day, he would be away the night, returning in the morning.

There was a seat near the top of the island backed by some furze bushes, and as Mrs ------- was busy with the household tasks the dressmaker took her work to the seat, anticipating a happy morning. But she felt strange and restless, and kept thinking she heard someone behind her, so she returned to the house and brought the little child back with her for company. After a short time the child also became restless, and then began to cry, saying she 'must go back to mammie' so they returned to the house. The day wore away without further incident, a large amount of sewing was accomplished and she was pleased with her days work.

About 9pm they retired, both sleeping in the same bed and the children in a cot in the same room. After sleeping soundly for some hours she was suddenly awakened – she heard no noise, but sleep entirely left her. The room had but one door, beside the bed: nor was there any cupboard or recess, but just plain walls. Gradually, opposite the bed a bluish light appeared and the figure of a man emerged out of the wall, a very tall, aristocratic looking man with grey hair, and he had very beautiful hands with long fingers (she noticed this particularly). He slowly crossed the room, the bluish light surrounding him like a haze, and went through the opposite wall. She was almost paralysed with fright and lay awake until the dawn broke. She did not awaken Mrs ------- (the baby had been fractious the early part of the night and the mother was sleeping heavily), but when it was light enough she got up, dressed, went downstairs, finding everything in order and all just the same as before going to bed. It was, she avers, no dream, but an apparition, and after so many years she can still see all in memory as she saw it then.

On Mr --------'s return she said she must go back. They were surprised and asked her reason. She would not tell them what she saw, but insisted on returning: nor could they persuade her to stay. It was a very long time before she visited the island again, and never did she sleep there again. She heard from several people that a bluish light was seen at intervals on the island, but never met anyone who had seen the ghost.

Some years afterwards a skeleton was dug up quite close to the seat. It was found to be that of a tall man with very long fingers. Possibly a body might have floated to the island from a wreck in the years gone by and been buried by whoever lived there then – or it may have been evidence of foul play.

Chapter 13

FLORA & FAUNA

Thanks to the Atkins sisters the island has been carefully conserved and it enjoys the benefit of a virtually frost-free climate. The following listing of plants and birds seen on the island was compiled by the sisters and does not pretend to be definitive but illustrates the diversity of wild life attracted by the climate and location.

Birds:

Blackbird
Bullfinch
Carrion Crow
Chiffchaff (S)
Cormorant
Dunlin (W)
Goldfinch
Grasshopper Warbler
Great Black Backed gull (approx. 15 pairs)
Greenfinch
Hedge Sparrow
Herring gull (approx. 450 pairs)

Herring Gull

House Sparrow
Jackdaw
Lesser Black Backed gull
Linnet
Mallard
Oystercatcher
Pied Wagtail
Purple Sandpiper (W)
Robin
Rock Pippit
Sanderling (W)
Shag
Song Thrush
Swallow (S)
Swift (S)
Turnstone
Whimbrel (P)
Whinchat (P)
Whitethroat (S)
Willow Warbler (S)
Wood Pigeon
Wren

Turnstone

Key: P = Passage migrant
            S = Summer visitor
            W = Winter visitor

Choughs once frequented the island and, earlier still, Puffins were to be seen there. Today, it is probable that Little Egrets visit the island since a colony of these attractive white members of the Heron family normally associated with the Mediterranean countries is now established on the Looe River.

Plants:

Beach

Burdock
Common Red Poppy
Fat Hen
Sea Beet
Sea Plantain
Sea Rocket

Common poppy
Papaver rhoeas

Thomas Bond, in his 1823 history of East and West Looe wrote that "Looe Island and the cliffs about Looe produce vast quanities of Samphire and Sea Pinks." Rock Samphire is still well established on the rocks and cliffs of East Looe today but there is little evidence of it on the island itself.

Cliff Top

Common Knotgrass
Common Mallow
English Stonecrop
Everlasting Pea
Hairy Tare
Sea Campion
Thick Leaved Stonecrop
Thrift

Sea campion
Silene maritima

Grassland & Hedgerow

Blackberry
Blueberry
Broad Leaved Dock
Coltsfoot
Dandelion
Common Vetch
Creeping Cinquefoil
Creeping Thistle
Cut-leaved Crane's-bill
Curled Dock
Daisy
Cermander Speedwell
Goosegrass
Greater Broad Leaved Plantain
Grey Field Speedwell
Groundsel
Hairy Hawkbit
Herb Robert
Horseshoe Vetch
Lady's Bedstraw
Lesser Bindweed
Meadow Buttercup
Nettle
Perennial Sow-thistle
Prickly Lettuce
Ragwort
Ribwort Plantain

Common Vetch

Prickly Lettuce

Rough Hawkbit
Scarlet Pimpernel
Self Heal
Silverweed
Sorrel
Spotted Medick
White Clover

Grasses:

Annual Meadow Grass
Cocksfoot
Creeping Bent
Crested Dogstail

False Oat Grass
Perennial Rye Grass
Rough Meadow Grass
Sheep's Fescue

Woodland:

Bracken
Chickweed
Common Gorse
Dog's Mercury
Elder
Foxglove
Fig Tree
Fumitory

Sorrel

Fumitory

Primrose
Red Campion
Royal Fern
Solomon's Seal
Sweet Chestnut
Sycamore
Violet
Wall Pennywort
Willow
Wood Garlic
Woody Nightshade
Yarrow

Hairy violet
Viola hirta

Animals:

As yet no attempt has been made to identify and list the animals on the island although it is interesting to note that a Roe Deer has been seen as recently as 2003, presumably having swum from the mainland in search of 'greener grass'! Seals are sometimes seen on the seaward side of the island.

BIBLIOGRAPHY & REFERENCES

Bibliography:

Alberry, Robert. *Talland Church* [Guide booklet]. Looe 1996

Atkins, Evelyn A. *We Bought an Island*. London: George G. Harrap Ltd., 1976

Atkins, Evelyn A. *Tales from our Cornish Island*. London: Harrap Ltd., 1986

Bond, Thomas. *Topographical and Historical Sketches of East and West Looe*, 1823

Chope, R. Pearse. *Early Tours in Devon & Cornwall*. Newton Abbott: David & Charles, 1967 (reprint with introduction by Alan Gibson).

Collins, Wilkie. *Rambles Beyond the Railway*. 1851

Correll, Philip. Diaries of John Cooke Harding and Mary Harding for September 1812 to February 1818. Philip Correll, 1993.

Derriman, James P. *Some Sources for the Maritime History of Cornwall (17th to 19th centuries)*. 1988

Dobson, Rev. C.C. *Did Our Lord Visit Cornwall – as they say in Cornwall and Somerset?* London: Covenant Publishing Ltd.1962 reprint.

Falkus, Christopher. *The Spanish Armada*. London: Pan Books Ltd.

Gibbons, Gavin. *Cornwall and the Isles of Scilly*. London: Geographia Ltd

Gilbert; *The Parochial History of Cornwall*, Vol. IV. 1938

Glover, J.E.B. *Place Names of Cornwall*.

Graham, Frank. *Smuggling in Cornwall*. Newcastle upon Tyne: V. Graham, 1964

Halliday, F.E. *A Story of Looe Island*. 1966

Hals & Tonkins. *The Parochial History of Cornwall*. 1838

Holmes, Julyan. *1,000 Cornish Place-Names Explained.*. Redruth: Truran Publications, 1983

Hunt, J. Roger. *A Story of Looe Island*. Ilfracombe, Devon: Arthur H. Stockwell Ltd., 1966

Johns, Jeremy Rowett. *Polperro's Smuggling Story*. Polperro Heritage Press, 1994

Johns, Jeremy Rowett, *The Smugglers' Banker*, Polperro Heritage Press, 1997

Leggat, P.O. & D.V. *A Tale of Two Mediaeval Chapels in Lammana Parish (Looe)*.1998 revision

Lewis, Rev. H.A. *The Child Christ at Lammana*. 2nd edition.

Lewis, Rev. H.A. *Christ in Cornwall*. 1936

Moore, Peter & Lister, Martin. *The Good Looe Story*. Liskeard, Cornwall: Peter Moore Publications, 1977

Newcombe, Lisa. *Smuggling in Cornwall & Devon* . Norwich: Jarrold & Sons Ltd., 1975

Noall, Cyril & Farr, Grahame. *Cornish Shipwrecks*. Tor Mark Press

Olson, Lynette. *Early Monasteries in Cornwall*. Wadebridge: The Boydell Press, 1989

Padel, O.J. *Cornish Place Names*. Penzance: Alison Hodge, 1988

Rockley, Veronica & Susan. *A Brief Biography of a Looe Smuggler*.

Rowse, A.L. *Tudor Cornwall*. Redruth: Dyllansow Truran. 1941

Shore, Commander Henry N. *Smuggling days and Smuggling Ways*. Philip Allen & Co Ltd, London, 1929

Vivian, John. *Tales of the Cornish Wreckers*. Truro, Cornwall: Tor Mark Press.

Wallis, John – *Vicar of Bodmin*. The Cornwall Register. 1847

Ward Lock. *Looe and South Cornwall*. London: Ward Lock & Co. Ltd, c. 1948

Waugh, Mary. *Smuggling in Devon & Cornwall 1700 - 1850*

References:

Cornish Times, The. Newspaper

Mayow of Bray. Two 18th c. indentures in Cornwall Record Office, Truro

Picken, W.W.M. *Light of Lammana*. Devon & Cornwall Notes & Queries 35 (1982), viii (1985)

Shapcott, Miss Elizabeth S. *A Little Looe Smuggling and a Few Looe Ghosts* published in *Old Cornwall*, Vol. 1, No.8, October 1928

Shaw, Rev. Stebbing. *A Tour to the West of England*, 1788

Shore, Commander H.N. *A Famous Smuggling Craft. The Cornish Magazine,* Vol. II, 1899.

Trelawny, Harriett. Diaries June 1873-August 1884

APPENDIX 1

Chronological listing of references to owners, residents and events:

From 1841 the national census, conducted every ten years, included the names of persons recorded plus their age and occupation. This provides us with another source of information about who was on the island, either resident or visiting, at the time.

The following chronological listing of references to owners and residents incorporates some of the available census returns:-

c. 1085   Chapel built on island.

1144   The island belonged to Glastonbury Abbey until 1289.

1200   "I Hastustus, son of Iohannes de Solenneio, have granted and by the present charter have confirmed to God and the church of the Blessed Virgin Mary of Glastonbury and to the convent of the same place the whole island of St. Michael of Lammana with all its appurtenances, both lands and tithes, which they hold from the ancient gift of my predecessors…."

1377   Island uninhabited according to a surviving record.

c. 1534   Island chapel endowed as a chantry chapel by a family called Courtenay.

1547/48	The suppression of chantries by Henry VIII would have closed the island and mainland chapels. The last known illustration of the island chapel is in Lysons' *Magna Britannia* and based upon a chart in the British Museum produced during Henry's reign.
1600	Sir John Trelawny purchased the Trelawne estate from the Crown.
1727	John Vening born (see family pedigree p.106).
16th c to 1729	Mayow of Bray
1729	Philip Mayow sold to his son and heir apparent, Burthogge Mayow.
1730	Burthogge Mayow sells to Benjamin Salmon.
1743	Island purchased by Governor Edward Trelawny, MP for West Looe in 1724 and again in 1727. Edward had a distinguished career and was appointed a Commissioner of Customs in 1732. He was Governor of Jamaica 1736-1752.
1775	The Trelawny estate, including the island, passed to Sir Harry Trelawny (7th baronet).
1781/3	A man [Finn/Fynn?] left Mewstone to his daughter and her three children (she had recently been widowed when her husband drowned) and moved to Looe Island.
1783 - 1823+	According to Bond in his 1823 book, island inhabited by one family from the Mewstone named Finn for about 40 years past.
1788	Owned by Sir Harry Trelawny and inhabited by Finn.
1790	Jochabed Hooper born 28th April to Anthony and Elizabeth Hooper of Looe Island

Sir Harry Trelawny

1793	One house on island inhabited by an old man and lady [his wife?] and family of eight in total including some grandchildren.
1795	Amram Hooper born 21st November to Anthony and Elizabeth Hooper of Looe Island [Talland records state Amram and Jochabed Hooper were baptised 25/06/1800]. The Godfathers were Revd William Hosker, George Blewett, John Penrise Esq and William Beard. The Godmothers; Mary Kendall, Amelia Kendall and Margaret Hext.. The Vicar was Charles Kendall.

The Parish records for Talland are deposited in the Cornwall Records Office, Truro, and are accompanied by a note, probably written by the Rev. Timberlake in the 1940s:

"The fullness of the entry is quite unique for the period, and the inclusion of names of Godparents of the latter, all with the possible exception of William Beard, who could be 'Marine of West Looe', are certainly county gentry – Kendals of Polsu intermarried with the Hext of Lanlivery. Revd W. Hosker (snr) was Rector of Lanteglos-by-Fowey from 1805, his son or grandson Vicar of Talland 1844 – 1858. I have tried to trace… and only find that Amram married Philippa Medland in 1823; they had a son, Benjamin (born 1823), who married (1857) Fanny Shapcott Honey, both then of West Looe – no trace of issue. Both Amram and Benjamin are detailed as 'Fishermen'."

1815	Elizabeth Hooper aged 54 loses her son, Benjamin Christopher, by drowning - aged 30
1817	One family resident on island according to C.S.Gilbert's *Survey of Cornwall* (1817)
1823	Amram Hooper married Philippa Medland at Talland church. Benjamin Hooper born to Amram and Philippa.
1827	Hooper and boy arrested at Fowey according to former smuggler.
1830's	Island said to be inhabited by an old man 'Hamram' and his daughter, Tilda. At this time Amram would have been 44.

A Coastguard was posted to the island at about this time in an attempt to prevent smuggling.

1830's   *Wisdom Penaluna* quoted in a 1901 article as saying the government resolved on planting a station on the island [to counter smuggling], close to the Hooper's farmhouse. He described it as a cottage surrounded by a ring wall [Smuggler's Cottage?] He said the farmhouse was old, ramshackle and surrounded by barns and outhouses but had since been pulled down and a new house built on the site. Since we know a coastguard was on the island at the time of the 1841 census (and presumably resident) it seems probable that the period referred to is prior to 1841.

Looe Island before the development of Hannafore
and completion of the Banjo Pier

1841   Census:

	AGE	OCCUPATION
Elizabeth Hooper	80	Independent means
Elizabeth Lane	55	Ditto
Matilda Bartlett	25	Ditto
Thomas Bartlett	10	Ditto
James Gallaway	40	Coastguard
Robert Gallaway	15	

The census enumerator records there were two houses and six inhabitants

1847   Cornwall Register gives population of Looe Island as six persons.

1851   Census:

	AGE	OCCUPATION	BIRTHPLACE
William Vague	30	Farmer-10 acres-one labourer	Pelynt
Jane Vague*	23		Gerrans
Ann Vague	1		Looe Island
Thos Wakeham	10	Farm Servant	Pelynt
Bridget Croon (widow)	67	House Servant [Jane's mother]	Gerrans
John Connor (married)	38	Commissioned boatman **	Cadgwith
William Climo (visitor)	7	Mariner's son at Coastguard Watch Hse.	Polruan

*nee' Coon [spelt Croon in the 1851 Census return]
** Coastguard Watch House
NB. The census enumerator reported that there was one dwelling house on the island and a temporary Watch House attached to the Looe Coast Guard Station. John Connor and William Climo were in the Watch House. Since we know the original farmhouse was demolished the reference to two houses in the 1841 Census and only one in 1851 suggests that today's house ('Island House') was built after 1851. The island was described as 'extra parochial' in 1851 i.e. not in a parish.

In Back Street, Looe we find the following in the 1851 census:-

	AGE	OCCUPATION	BIRTHPLACE
Amram Hooper	56	Fisherman	Looe Island
Philippa Hooper	52		W. Looe
Benjamin Hooper	24	Fisherman	E. Looe
Philippa Hooper	15		E. Looe

1853   Birth on Looe Island of John Vague, son of William and Jane Vague (née Coon) on 26th May.

1861   Census

	AGE	OCCUPATION	BIRTHPLACE
William Vague	41	Farming 15 acres – employing 1 man	born Pelynt
Jane Vague	31	Wife	born St. Germans
Ann Vague	11	Daughter	born Island of St. George
Mary J Vague	10	ditto	ditto
John Vague	7	Son	ditto
Emma Vague	5	Daughter	ditto
Elizabeth Vague	2	ditto	ditto
James Much (?)	17	Servant – Agricultural Labourer	born Pelynt

1871

At the time of the 1871 census the enumerator wrote: *Advertisements have been placed to builders or contractors for the erection of a cottage on the island.*

The Vague family had moved to the mainland:

	AGE	OCCUPATION	BIRTHPLACE
William Vague	52	Farmer 30 acres	Pelynt
Jane	42		Gerrans

Elizabeth	80	Widowed mother -son supports	Holsworthy, Devon
John Vague	17		Looe Island
Ann Maria Vague	15	Scholar	Looe Island
Elizabeth Vague	12	Scholar	Looe Island

1873/1876   According to the diary of Harriet Trelawny 'Lewis [Sir William Lewis Salusbury-Trelawny] took possession of Looe Island' on the 3rd January. Harriet also mentions trees being planted there in 1873, and inspecting the site for a house to be built there on 27th January 1876.

1877   James Henry Nicholls and his wife were installed on the island, 18th November 1876, in the employ of Mr Trelawny who kept two boats there. Their tenure was preceded by one Cranford who left on the same day according to Harriet Trelawny. She also mentions sheep and hens being kept on the island, catching rabbits and cutting hay.

1881   Census:

	AGE	OCCUPATION	BIRTHPLACE
James Nicholas	31	Keeper of Island	W. Looe
Mary J Nicholas	31	Keeper's wife	Morval

1883   C.H. Leycester rented the island from Mr Neale of Bristol for four years. Sadly, he was drowned on a fishing trip together with his wife and niece.

1885   Sir William Lewis Salusbury-Trelawny inherited from his father Sir John

1891   Census:-

	AGE	OCCUPATION	BIRTHPLACE
Alfred Walters	26	Keeper of the Island	Penryn
Minnie Walters	26		Plymouth
Isabble [sic] Emma Job	17	Sister-in-law	Buckland, Devon

1894   A court case reveals that Ezra Joseph Neale, a potato merchant of 24 Thomas Street, Bristol had been lessee of the island for 15 years. His caretaker, who lived on the island with his wife, was Joseph Williams, a naval pensioner [engaged 1893]

1894   Body of Thomas Bartlett Bowden found off Gorran Haven [*Cornish Times* 6th October 1894]

Looe Island from the mainland (1912) showing a much smaller wooded area than today

1912	About this time Henry St. John Dix Esq took on a 21 year lease expiring June 1933
	Lease assigned R.J. Ward to J.W. Topham 30/06
	Mortgage 29/03 J.W. Topham to L.A.L. North
	25/05 – Sir J.W.S Trelawny and Equity & Law Life Ass Socy
	04/07 – Conveyance Sir J.W.S. Trelawny & Anor to Mrs E. Topham
	07/07 – Conveyance Mrs E. Topham & Others to P. Corder

The ownership and occupation of the island between 1914 and 1921 is confusing. A schedule of documents and deeds refers to an assignment 30th June 1914 'R.J. Ward to J.W. Topham' and a mortgage 29th March 1921, 'J.W. Topham to L.A.L. North'. Then on the 25th May 1921 a 'Consent to Sale', 'Sir J.W.S. Trelawny and Equity & Law Life Ass. Socy. A conveyance on 4th July 1921, 'Sir J. Trelawny & Another to Mrs E. Topham' is followed a few days later [07/07/1921] by a conveyance 'Mrs E. Topham & Others to P. Corder.

1921	Looe Island sold
1923	Directory of Cornwall says Looe Island is the property of Paul Corder Esq. and formerly extra-parochial
1943	08/06 – Conveyance Miss D. C. Corder to C. Kingerlee
1949	21/01 – C. Kingerlee to Mrs A. L. Kenward
1952	25/03 – Mrs A.L. Kingerlee to Major Gen. S.B. Rawlins

1957	02/07 – Persons Representing Gen S.B. Rawlins deceased to Trustees of Mr & Mrs C.H. Whitehouse's Marriage Settlement
1964	22/10 – R. Coop & Others to Misses R.A. & E.E. Atkins

APPENDIX 2

Shipwrecks

A selective list of shipwrecks on, or in the vicinity of, St. George's Island with the date of loss..

SHIP	DATE/EVENT
Wolf	December 1691
Ellis	December 1751 with a cargo of tin
Speedwell	January 1786
Tregothick	January 1786 in Talland Bay
Unanimity	29th December 1802 on the rocks between St. George's Island and Hannafore carrying best 'Rose Cork' butter from Cork to London. The vessel was a Sloop in the command of Capt. Smith.
Rose	23rd January 1809 near St. George's Island en route from Plymouth to Falmouth under command of Capt. Knight. The crew of 26 were all drowned and the stern frame was washed up near Looe the following day.
Harmonie	22nd November 1824 in a storm - crew lost.

Jane December 1827 probably lured into trouble by wreckers.

Hart 8th August 1828. Went aground on St. George's Island whilst sailing from Plymouth to Fowey with a cargo of Limestone. The crew of two men and one boy were saved.

Konigsberg 1834

Bellissima November 1838.

Dart 15th July 1842. This Brig (net tonnage 123) went down off St. George's Island carrying a cargo of Limestone. There were no fatalities.

Incentive 1st October 1863. Schooner built in 1838 with a gross tonnage of 73 foundered on Looe Island under the command of Capt. Cock.

Albion 23rd November 1872 on rocks near St. George's Island.

Rosehill 23rd September 1917 – steamship torpedoed by German 'U' boat.

Zarita 27th May 1926 – Steam ketch sailing from Plymouth to Genoa became stranded on Magmain rocks west of Looe and wrecked. The crew of four were saved by lifeboat.

Silent 8th May 1827 – fishing vessel from Brixham in collision in fog off St. George's Island with a Dutch vessel and sank. The crew of three were saved by the Dutch vessel.

Naiad 28th March 1931 – Schooner wrecked in gale on rocks just south west of Looe having dragged anchor whilst waiting to enter harbour with a cargo of granite. The pilot boat saved the crew.

APPENDIX 3

THE LAST OF THE SMUGGLERS – an interview

"That there telegraph was the end o' we. It killed honest trade." With these words an old smuggler concluded his tale of the good old times of 'free trade'.

He is aged 96, a Cornishman; still able, as he assured me, to do as good day's work as can any young man of the present generation. I had come on him after he had spent a day in the harvest field, and there most certainly binding sheaves and in tossing into the wagon he kept pace with men fifty years his junior.

He has never married. "My sister" said he "her kep house for me sixty year; and when her died, I were too old to marry – leastways, I reckon the maidens 'ud say so." "Have you asked any?" He shook his head. "I didn't want to be made a fule of – by one takin me."

Wisdom Penaluna – I do not give his real name, as I am not sure he would like it – spent a twelvemonth in prison the year King William was crowned. "All along o' free trade" as he explained. In fact, he had been caught smuggling. That was in 1830, consequently when he was a lusty young fellow of twenty-six. "Then'm was brave times" said Penanluna. "What? When in prison?." "No – out of it," he answered sharply. "Tea sold in England at eight shillings a pound and we could buy in Guernsey or Jersey at sevenpence. That was tidy profits. The year of the breaking out of the Revolution in France (1830) I was over at Cherbourg, and I and my mate we bought a score of tubs of Hollands – that is to say, twenty-one to the score – for seven pounds. We brought them back safe to England and sold them for three guineas a tub. Made by that transaction £26. That's what I call fair trading. We got 'baccy at Jersey for sevenpence a pound, same as tea, and sold it at half-a-crown. That weren't quite the profits as there was on tea, but it was easier to dispose of. And one-and-eleven on a pound ain't to be sneezed at."

The old man smiled; his face glowed with conscious pride. Not a shadow of a suspicion that there was anything of blame, morally, attaching to his conduct passed over his conscience. I am quite sure he reckoned up his successful runs with contraband goods as some men count up their good deeds.

"At times," continued he, "there was rough dealings. I mind in February 1816 there was a bit of a scratch. The chaps had brought over a famous lot o' spirits and got all safe ashore. The Customs men heard of it somehow, and two riding officers came out and called to their aid two light horsemen, and tried to stop the goods being carried from the shore to the distributing place. But the farmers all round came to the aid of the smugglers and there was some fighting. One officer was thrown from his horse and had an arm broken; some of our men were severely wounded. Search was made for them after the affair, but they were not to be found; they'd been hid away, and were kept hid till their wounds were healed. I reckon there was a hundred and fifty men out that day – our fellows and the farmers and their men."

"I suppose you were not always successful?" "No; I were cotched that year George IV died [1830]. The worst of it was, we had to do with informers. The Government they had paid spies everywhere; they had spies in France, they had spies on our own Cornish coast – more shame to Cornishmen for doing the dirty work! But, bless you sir! There will always be tares among the wheat; we are told that in Scriptur.'"

Then the old fellow flushed up, reared himself, and said – "Did you ever hear of the Hoopers of Looe Island?"

"Never"

"Well, the first o' the Hoopers was a banished man to the Mewstone off Plymouth. Why he wor sent there I cannot tell; but if he were to be ketched ashore on the mainland, he'd ha' been hung. So he lived till he died on the Mewstone, and there the Hooper I knowed and will tell 'ee about he were reared. The Hooper I knowed he left the Mewstone, and takin' kindly-like to an island, he took to living on Looe Island – that's about eight acres, and off the coast of Looe; it belongs to Sir William Trelawny – always did belong to the Trelawnys, ever sin' it wor created. He gave ten shillin' an acre for the island; in all four pound. I hear tell it lets now for forty or fifty. Hooper, he and his sister, Black Till they called her, and a boy, they lived there. Black Till was the clever one. Sometimes her dressed as a man, and her'd work like a sailor but she'd put on petticoats sometimes – Easter

Day, like enough. There was once a black man on that island – his head has been found and put in a glass case now. But there! – I'm ramblin' away. Hooper and the boy went over to Roscoff in a fourteen feet boat and brought away a lading of tubs. T'were cruel rough weather, and they was balin' all night long to keep the open boat afloat. They couldn't make Looe Island, so they runned into the mouth of Fowey Harbour, and up a little creek to the mill. They was that terrible tired out that they crep' into the straw in the barn and fell dead asleep. I reckon that was in 1827. What do 'ee think now of the miller? He went off same night and betrayed 'em, and Hooper and the boy was took sleep-drunk as they lay in the straw, and all the tubs were seized. What do 'ee think now should be done wi' such a villain as that there miller? Hangin' would be too good for the likes of he!"

"What did become of him?" I asked.

"Well you see there be providence over all; and the face of Heaven turned agin him after that, and he never prospered, but went down, down."

"I suppose the good folk gave up dealing with him?"

"Aye; 'twas so, I reckon. A chap as acted as did he, all the honest men were agin him, and he wor lucky that he didn't get trun'led over the cliffs."

A pause and then –

"I reckon he knowed it mightn't be over safe for her to go along the edge o' the cliffs after that."

As mention has been made of Roscoff – a little place in Brittany that flourished on the illicit trade with Cornwall, and has languished since that trade has ceased – it may be mentioned that there was a notorious man of the name Coppinger, who had a small estate near St. Austell, and another at Roscoff. He had a lugger of his own, and during the European war was employed by the British Government to convey communications between

England and France. The man was well known to be engaged in contraband trade, and it is for that reason that he was received with suspicion in a French port. Of course, during the war the French were only too willing to damage British revenue by the encouragement of smuggling. But the English Government, knowing the man to be a smuggler, connived at his proceedings for the sake of having a means of carrying on secret communication with their agents in the enemy's country.

Coppinger must have done well, for he married a daughter of a Trefusis, son of Lord Clinton, and a son married the daughter of Sir John Murray, Baronet, of Stanhope. On the occasion of the marriage of his daughter, he gave her as a portion the sum of £40,000.

To return to the Hoopers.

As already said, they had a house on Looe Island. This became an emporium for smuggled goods. The brother and sister were so clever and so daring that the revenue officers were continually baulked by them. At last the Government resolved on planting a station upon the island itself, close to the farmhouse of the Hoopers, where it was to be as a cat watching a mouse. It was a cottage surrounded by a ring wall [Smuggler's Cottage?].

The farmhouse was old, ramshackle, and was surrounded with barns and outhouses. The house itself has since been pulled down and a new one built on its site.

As the island grew nothing but rabbits, it was obvious that these outbuildings could only be used for merchandise, not for agricultural produce. The boy was now employed to watch the one preventative man who was planted to watch the farm. All the business done was done when the officer was asleep. The lively traffic of the Hoopers was hampered, not stopped.

On one occasion a smuggling vessel ran boldly to the island and discharged her cargo. The one preventative officer could not approach. A ring of men kept him at a distance. However, the proceeding had been observed from the shore, and a preventative boat was manned and run out, but did not reach the island till the vessel had spread sails and departed.

The premises of the Hoopers was searched – nothing was to be found. Black Till sat over the fire smoking; Hooper himself stood listless, with his hands in his pockets. The officers ransacked the barn, the outhouses, every portion of the dwelling – and found nothing. They could swear that the ship had discharged run-goods, and nothing savouring of contraband was to be detected. Annoyed and angry, they departed.

In fact, there were numerous subterranean passages, so carefully concealed that to the present day only one has been discovered, and that by the giving way of a portion of the floor of the barn.

Now, although the smack had landed her cargo, there was another proceeding to be gone through before the cargo was safe. It had to be conveyed to the mainland.

One day Black Till ran in despair to the preventative man, with tears in her eyes and wringing her hands.

"Oh, lor!" cried she, "what iver shall us do? There is our boat hev broke away, and be now carried out to say. Do'ee now help me, there's a dear man. If that 'ere boat be lost, I'll go drowned myself."

The obliging officer ran to the cliff and saw the black speck of the boat tossing on the waves, and being swept out to sea by the tide. He at once jumped into his own boat and rowed hard in pursuit of her, and after some time succeeded in recovering her.

Whilst this was going on one side of the island, a party of smugglers was clearing the hiding-place and carrying away the tubs of spirits as fast as they could on shore. The officer returned, bringing the rescued boat with him. Whether he ever found out how he had been befooled I could not learn.

Method of Slinging Tubs

At one time the officer who patrolled the shore at Looe was in the pay of the smugglers. He rode a white or grey cob. On reaching Looe, a man would come up to him and say "That's a nice cob you have; is he for sale?" "That depends," the officer would answer. "I ain't inclined to sell him dirt cheap."

After a little haggling a price was agreed on. Then the officer would say, "Now, I can't walk home, you see, so you must lend me the cob for my return."

And the officer persistently watched the vegetation on the banks and the inland landscape as he rode home, and never by any chance cast a look at the sea. That cob was believed to have been sold over half-a-hundred times. The story was told me that when old Hooper lay a-dying he was offered as much as sixty pounds if he would reveal the secret of the hiding-place. He steadfastly refused. "I'll die as I lived – an honest man," he said.

The farmers were in league with the 'free traders'. As soon as it was made known to them that a vessel was about to discharge in the nearest cove, they would assemble their men. The farmers kept donkeys, which were ostensibly employed to carry loads of sand from the beach for the manuring of the fields. On the occasion of the landing of a cargo these donkeys were put into requisition. But the men were all accustomed to carry kegs. Indeed, at Cherbourg, Roscoff, and elsewhere, the 'tubs' of brandy were provided suitably furnished with slings. These slings consisted of a piece of small rope secured round each end of the tub, so as to leave the two 'tails' of rope of equal length. A cargo was not always carried on board a vessel, but was frequently sunk and towed, and when so, a chain of tubs was formed by tying one of the sling-ropes to the sinking rope. When the 'crop' was brought ashore the rope end was untied or cut, and then the tub carriers took one tail over each shoulder, and tied other tails together. Thus each man carried two tubs.

When a smuggling vessel towed a number of tubs a heavy stone was slung between each, so as to keep them under water and invisible. Moreover, on reaching the coast, if it were not possible to at once remove the 'crop', it was customary to sink it. This was done by fastening each rope end to a small anchor, which prevented the crop from drifting away. Then the smugglers could take their own time to remove the sunken spirits. The revenue officers were, however, well aware of this, and if they had observed a suspicious-looking vessel moving about the coast, and then run in they would feel or 'creep' for the cargo with crooks, and raise the sunken kegs if able to light on them.

Signals at night were given with flint and steel. A code of flashes was agreed upon. Also windows that commanded the sea were eminently useful as a means of communication. The smugglers had their agents on shore shadowing the preventive men, and they had a lingo of their own, by means of which they were able to give information, even before their enemies, without being understood. Whistling certain tunes was also a means of conveying instructions or giving a warning. 'Jenny to the Fair' meant that the coast was clear; 'Balaam' was a caution that watch was kept. Along the coast at various points were – and still are – places of concealment. They are now no longer used for contraband goods, and people are not shy of pointing them out. Among the many that exist may be mentioned the 'Vouga', near Penrose, in the parish of St. Eval. There is a valley that runs down to a small cove, with a beach. Opening out of this valley is a lateral coombe – all moor – covered with heather, gorse, and brambles. In the side of this coombe, hidden behind briars, is the mouth of a cave that has been cut out of the rock. It forms a passage or gallery, and has marks in the side where a door and beams were placed to secure the entrance. A lateral gallery is said to have run a mile underground, and to open into the back yard of a cottage on the cliffs. Much of this has fallen in, but both entrances remain, and the places where the roof has given way can also be traced. There are still alive people who can recall when this was used.

"'Ah, sir," said my man to me, "in them glorious days us didn't count gold, us measured it out."

I have seen a china imperial quart mug in which the gold was thus measured. At Maker there lived a handsome woman – she is now dead –who used to go up and down the street, carrying a baby in long clothes. One day a preventative man in passing greeted her – "Well, Mrs Lee, a quiet baby yours – never cries!" "No. I reckon her don't cry terrible, but her's got a lot o'spirit, for all that, in her."

And so the 'baby' had. It was a keg of brandy.

It was a favourite practice to press well known smugglers for the navy. One such was thus taken and run on board a man-o-war lying in Cawsand Bay. He waited his time. One evening, when he thought the opportunity was come, he jumped overboard and swam to a fishing-smack anchored hard by, cut her adrift, and hoisted sail.

The wind blew strong inshore, and he was speedily making for land. The alarm was given and a boat sent in pursuit. The smuggler waited until he got near another boat, then again went overboard, and watched the man-o-war's men rowing in pursuit of the empty smack, which, with sail spread, ran ashore. When he deemed himself safe he made for the land in another direction, and was never re-taken. The man died a few years ago. The condition of mind in which the State is regarded as the natural enemy, to be resisted, overreached, defrauded, is not one which we can at present readily comprehend. And yet it is quite possible that such a condition of mind may again occur should the State unduly tax and oppress any class by laying excessive burdens, upon it; or, again, should it become so Socialistic in its all-embracing activity as to threaten individualism with extinction.

It was a favourite belief among the smugglers that the Customs duties were laid on goods by the Government for the purpose of maintaining a fleet to protect the shores of Great Britain from the incursions of Algerine pirates. The necessity ceased, yet the Customs were maintained. The smugglers justified themselves by pretending that the Government had not kept faith with the nation, and that in consequence no moral obligation weighed on them to respect the law in this matter."

The use of the island by smugglers was also described in an article by Henry Shore, *A Famous Smuggling Craft*, published in 1899. This includes an account of a smuggling trip in the 1830's that he claims was given by an old smuggler from Cawsand, near Plymouth, shortly before his death. This merits being reproduced in full because it graphically illustrates the hazards faced by the smugglers and the role of the island in their trade:-

"The only trip I ever made in the *Daniel and William* [a notorious smuggling vessel in the mid 1830's] was when Dan Maddocks was skipper; Chenoworth and John Dunstan were along with me. We were bound to Cherbourg for a cargo of sperrits [*sic*], in four-gallon tubs. It was all brandy what was brought over then – white brandy-but we called it sperrits, for it was a deal above proof; four gallons of sperrits would make six, with the right quantity of water and colouring matter along with it. And that was the stuff we took in.

We ran across from Cherbourg without any bother, shipped the goods, and made a try back. But the wind headed and blew up strong, so we had to run back and wait for a fair slant. The spot we were bound for was Looe Island, a nice quiet place, where you could land your goods and stow 'em away in caves without being interrupted, and get them run ashore to Looe afterwards, whenever the coast was clear of prewentivmen [sic]. It was just about this time that the coastguard got wind of the dodge, and set a couple of men to watch the island.

We had two Cawsand men waiting for us on shore, stowed away out of sight, so that the coastguard shouln't get wind of the affair. You see, in those days there was only one cottage on the island, in which an old man called Hamram, and his daughter 'Tilda lived. They had a cave somewhere, but no one ever found it; and they took jolly good care no one should see them put the tubs into it – they always sent the chaps inside the house while that was going on. They were staunch smugglers, both on 'em, and the goods would lie there safe enough till a chance offered to get 'em landed. They'd get a small sum for every tub they took care of – I don't think they ever got tubs brought across themselves – and that's how they made a living.

Well, we had to wait at Cherbourg some time before we got a proper slant of wind. At last we ran across with a regular gale from the south-east and anchored under the lee of the island about midnight. Now, that was the best of this spot – no matter which way the wind was you could always get shelter, one side or t' other; and after the goods was landed, why, we did'nt care. There was a tr'ble sea running, the craft was pitching bows under, and presently the anchor began to drag and we nearly druv ashore, as the cable ran right out to the clinch. Oh, it was a dre'ful night, to be sure. I made sartin we should have to swim for it.

After waiting for close on an hour, watching for the boat to come off, and seeing no signs of anyone, we launched our own, though she was little better than a dinghy, and set to work to land the tubs. My word, we had a job! But we got them all ashore without losing a tub. There was'nt a soul on the island, barring Hamram and 'Tilda – our chaps had gone home, thinking we'd run in to another spot to land. However, they soon got the tubs carried up with their donkey, and stowed away safe.

As it happened, things couldn't have turned out better for us. For although our two chaps weren't, we had the place all to ourselves. It was pay-day with the coastguards, and they'd all gone ashore to Looe, and it was blowing

so hard they couln't get off again that night. That was a good job for us! It was close to four o'clock in the morning before we got everything clear; and dre'ful work it was, in a devil of a sea, and with nothing but a small boat to land in. As it was, she pretty nigh got her bow knocked out of her, and she leaked so bad we had to pass a line round her to keep the planks together the last trip we made.

Directly everything was clear we shipped our cable and ran round to Plymouth – the wind had shifted, you see. But before we could get under weigh the boat had her bow pulled clean out of her and she drifted ashore somewhere by Downderry, I believe. Did I say we saved all the tubs? Well, then, I lied! For two were washed out of the boat while we were landing them, and were picked up afterwards by the coastguard on the beach near Looe.

When we were abreast of Cawsand we were boarded by Mr Foote, the officer stationed there, to search us for a double bottom [a false bottom to conceal tubs] – he'd information against us, you see. He found nothing, though, of course, he knew well enough what we'd been after. The fact was some one had informed against us, and if it hadn't been for the pay-day at Looe, and the boatman not being able to get off the island, we should have been nabbed, sure enough. Some of our friends had sent a boat across to Cherbourg with a letter telling us that information was out against us. We saw a boat pass, but took no notice of her, not knowing where it was bound to; and as the chaps aboard didn't know our craft we heard nothing of the affair till we got back. The man who informed was a labourer by name of Sparkes, living in Millbay, who had a lot of private places about the country, and made a good bit of money by keeping tubs for parties. He wanted to get into the revenue cutter, and so he gave information to the officer in Looe. However, he got nothing by it for, you see, we saved all our goods.

The morning after we'd landed the cargo the coastguard came to the island, almost before Hamram had properly cleared up his place after stowing away the tubs. You see, they had dead information against us, even if it hadn't been for their finding the boat and the two tubs we'd lost, and they searched and dug all over the island for days, but they found nothing. The tubs – there were three hundred of 'em – lay in the caves on Looe island for three months before there was a chance of running them.

Now that was the only trip I ever made in the *Daniel and William* but there's no doubt she was one of the most notorious smuggling craft on the coast.

Did I ever see the caves? No! Why, now, it would never have done to let people into the secret. It mightn't have mattered for once, but in the long run some blackguard would have been sure to have informed agin Hamram, and then the game would have been up. What's more, the caves never were found, the secret died along with 'em".

There is a sequel to this story; not long after the *Daniel and William'* was later seized by a revenue vessel, probably as the result of a tip-off from an informant in France, and towed to Fowey where she was sawn into three portions to punish the owners.

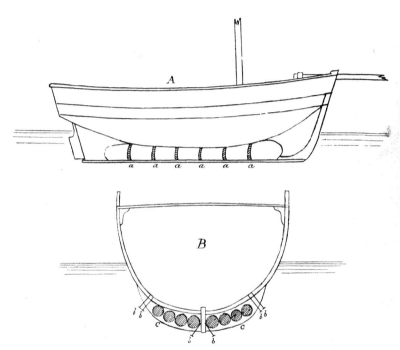

Contraband hidden in false bottom of the Daniel & William. [*The Cornish Magazine 1899*]

CONCEALMENT FITTED TO THE 'DANIEL AND WILLIAM'

APPENDIX 4

Elderflower 'Champagne'

The ingredients:

4 to 6 elderflower heads in full bloom
1.5lbs granulated sugar
2 lemons
2 tablespoons white vinegar
8 pints of water

To prepare:

Squeeze lemons and chop peel. Put all the ingredients in a clean bucket/bowl and stir until the sugar is dissolved.

Cover and leave for 24 hours. Strain (muslin is ideal) and pour into one pint beer bottles (or similar) leaving 2.5 inches headroom. Seal with plastic press-on caps (not screw caps).

The refreshing drink, which was a great favourite of the Atkins sisters, is ready in two weeks.

The Atkins sisters enjoying a glass of their 'Elderflower Champagne' at Jetty Cottage

APPENDIX 5

Descendants of Elizabeth VENING

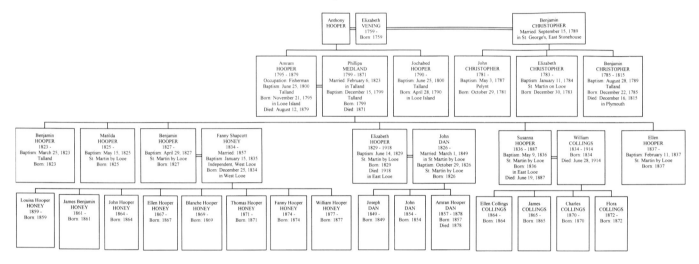

Anthony HOOPER	Elizabeth VENING 1759 - Born: 1759

Benjamin CHRISTOPHER
Married: September 15, 1789
in St. George's, East Stonehouse

Amram HOOPER
1795 - 1879
Occupation: Fisherman
Baptism: June 25, 1800
Talland
Born: November 21, 1795
in Looe Island
Died: August 12, 1879

Phillipa MEDLAND
1799 - 1871
Married: February 6, 1823
in Talland
Baptism: December 15, 1799
Talland
Born: 1799
Died: 1871

Jochabed HOOPER
1790 -
Baptism: June 25, 1800
Talland
Born: April 28, 1790
in Looe Island

John CHRISTOPHER
1781 -
Baptism: May 3, 1787
Pelynt
Born: October 29, 1781

Elizabeth CHRISTOPHER
1783 -
Baptism: January 11, 1784
St. Martin on Looe
Born: December 30, 1783

Benjamin CHRISTOPHER
1785 - 1815
Baptism: August 28, 1789
Talland
Born: December 22, 1785
Died: December 16, 1815
in Plymouth

Benjamin HOOPER
1823 -
Baptism: March 25, 1823
Talland
Born: 1823

Matilda HOOPER
1825 -
Baptism: May 15, 1825
St. Martin by Looe
Born: 1825

Benjamin HOOPER
1827 -
Baptism: April 29, 1827
St. Martin by Looe
Born: 1827

Fanny Shapcott HONEY
1834 -
Married: 1857
Independent, West Looe
Baptism: January 15, 1835
Born: December 25, 1834
in West Looe

Elizabeth HOOPER
1829 - 1918
Baptism: June 14, 1829
St. Martin by Looe
Born: 1829
Died: 1918
in East Looe

John DAN
1826 -
Married: March 1, 1849
in St Martin by Looe
Baptism: October 29, 1826
St. Martin by Looe
Born: 1826

Susanna HOOPER
1836 - 1887
Baptism: May 9, 1836
St. Martin by Looe
Born: 1836
in East Looe
Died: June 19, 1887

William COLLINGS
1834 - 1914
Born: 1834
Died: June 28, 1914

Ellen HOOPER
1837 -
Baptism: February 11, 1837
St. Martin by Looe
Born: 1837

Louisa Hooper HONEY
1859 -
Born: 1859

James Benjamin HONEY
1861 -
Born: 1861

John Hooper HONEY
1864 -
Born: 1864

Ellen Hooper HONEY
1867 -
Born: 1867

Blanche Hooper HONEY
1869 -
Born: 1869

Thomas Hooper HONEY
1871 -
Born: 1871

Fanny Hooper HONEY
1874 -
Born: 1874

William Hooper HONEY
1877 -
Born: 1877

Joseph DAN
1849 -
Born: 1849

John DAN
1854 -
Born: 1854

Amran Hooper DAN
1857 - 1878
Born: 1857
Died: 1878

Ellen Collings COLLINGS
1864 -
Born: 1864

James COLLINGS
1865 -
Born: 1865

Charles COLLINGS
1870 -
Born: 1870

Flora COLLINGS
1872 -
Born: 1872

*James Benjamin Hooper (left),
Amram Hooper's grandson*

INDEX

The Old Guildhall Museum and Gaol

High Market Street, East Looe, Cornwall

Lower floor dating from 1450. Upper floor (c1587) contains magnificent Magistrates' Bench and Royal Coat of Arms.

Open: Easter Week. Spring Bank Holiday until 30th September
11.30am – 4.30pm, Sunday – Friday
Adults: £1.50   Children: 50p

Exhibits include fishing, mining, history of Looe, particularly Victorian development, Looe Island and smugglers; hands-on exhibits for children.

For further information, contact the Curator
Barbara Birchwood-Harper 01503-262070 or 263709